Windows® 7
FOR
DUMMIES®
QUICK REFERENCE

by Greg Harvey

Wiley Publishing, Inc.

Windows® 7 For Dummies® Quick Reference

Published by
Wiley Publishing, Inc.
111 River Street
Hoboken, NJ 07030-5774

WILEY

About the Author

Greg Harvey, the author of a slew of *For Dummies* books running the gamut from *Excel For Dummies* to *The Origins of Tolkien's Middle-earth For Dummies*, has had a long career of teaching business people the use of IBM PC, Windows, and Macintosh software. From 1983 to 1988, he conducted hands-on computer software training for corporate business users with a variety of training companies (including his own, PC Teach). From 1988 to 1992, he taught university classes in Lotus 1-2-3 and Introduction to Database Management Technology (using dBASE) in the Department of Information Systems at Golden Gate University in San Francisco.

In mid-1993, Greg started a new multimedia publishing venture, Mind over Media, Inc. As a multimedia developer and computer book author, he hopes to enliven his future online computer books by making them into true interactive learning experiences that will vastly enrich and improve the training of users of all skill levels. In 2006, he received his PhD in Comparative Philosophy and Religion with a concentration on Asian Studies from the California Institute of Integral Studies in San Francisco, California. When he isn't busy writing, Dr. Greg works as a Healing Harp intern at Marin General Hospital with the Institute for Health and Healing and as a complimentary care volunteer playing harp for patients with the Hospice By The Bay in Larkspur, California.

Contents at a Glance

Table of Contents

Part 1

The Windows 7 User Experience

When fully utilized, the Windows 7 desktop, as shown in the following figure, offers an extremely rich, visual user experience. However, as you find out in this part, the Windows 7 desktop is much more than just a pretty face. Indeed, Windows 7 is also Microsoft's most powerful and usable personal computer interface to date (and this statement is coming from someone who really liked Windows XP — and Vista not so much).

In this part . . .

- ✔ **Getting Acquainted with the Windows 7 Desktop**
- ✔ **Adding Gadgets to Your Desktop**
- ✔ **Using the Getting Started Option and Windows Help and Support**
- ✔ **Personalizing the Windows 7 Desktop**
- ✔ **Using the Windows 7 Taskbar**

Desktop

The Windows 7 desktop (see Figure 1-1) consists of the taskbar (*see* "Taskbar" later in this part) that normally appears along the bottom of the screen, a background image (or color) that fills the rest of the screen (*see* "Personalize" later in this part), any gadgets you display on the screen (*see* "Gadgets" later in this part), and whatever desktop icons and desktop shortcuts you then choose to place on this background.

Recycle Bin desktop icon   Desktop background image   Gadgets ─┐

Figure 1-1

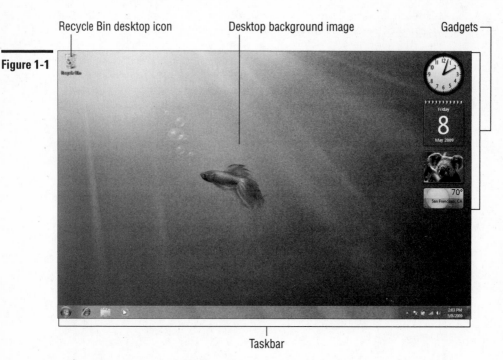

Taskbar

Displaying additional desktop icons

The Windows 7 desktop starts with just a single Recycle Bin desktop icon (where you drop any files, folders, and desktop shortcuts you want deleted from the system). In addition to the Recycle Bin icon, you can add the following icons to your Windows 7 desktop:

- **Computer:** To open your Computer window (same as choosing Start⇨ Computer from the taskbar), which shows all the drives and components connected to your computer (including drives that you've mapped onto a drive letter).

✔ **User's Files:** To open your Documents window (same as choosing Start⇨Documents from the taskbar), which shows all the document files on your computer. (**See** "Windows Explorer" in Part 2.)

✔ **Network:** To open the Network window (same as choosing Start⇨Network), which shows all the computers on your local area network. (**See** Part 3.)

✔ **Control Panel:** To open the Control Panel (same as Start⇨Control Panel), which enables you to customize all sorts of computer settings. (**See** "Control Panel" in Part 5.)

To add any or all of these desktop icons, follow these steps:

1. Right-click somewhere on the desktop background (not on any icon) and then choose Personalize from the shortcut menu that appears.

2. In the Personalization window that appears, click the Change Desktop Icons link in the Navigation pane to open the Desktop Icon Settings dialog box.

3. Click the check boxes for all the desktop icons (Computer through Control Panel) you want to appear on the Windows 7 desktop.

4. Click OK to close the Desktop Icons Settings dialog box and then click the Close button in the upper-right corner of the Personalization window.

After adding a desktop icon to the desktop, you can open its window by double-clicking the icon or right-clicking it and then choosing Open from its shortcut menu.

Creating desktop shortcuts

You can create desktop shortcuts to launch applications you've installed as well as to open drives, folders, documents on your computer system, and Web pages on the Internet.

To create a desktop shortcut, you need to do just two things:

1. Locate the icon for the program, drive, folder, or document for which you want to create the shortcut on the Start menu or in the Computer, Network, or Documents window. (To create a shortcut to a Web page, right-click the page in the Internet Explorer, click the Create Shortcut option on its shortcut menu, and click OK in the alert dialog box that asks whether you want the shortcut on your desktop.)

2. Right-click the program, folder, or document icon and then choose Send To⇨Desktop (Create Shortcut) on the icon's shortcut menu.

In the case of a Web page, choose File➪Send➪Shortcut to Desktop in Internet Explorer when the Classic pull-down menus are displayed.

Note that to create a desktop shortcut to a drive on your computer system, you must right-click the drive and choose the Create Shortcut item from its shortcut menu (there is no Send To item). Windows 7 then displays an alert dialog box indicating that it can't create a shortcut in the same window and asking whether you want the shortcut placed on the desktop instead. Click the Yes button.

You can also use a wizard to create a desktop shortcut by following these few steps:

1. Right-click anywhere on the desktop (but not on an existing desktop item) and then choose New➪Shortcut from the shortcut menu that appears.

2. Enter the location of the item to which you want to create the shortcut either by entering its path and filename or URL (Web) address or by clicking the Browse button and locating the item in the Browse for Files or Folders dialog box before you click OK.

3. Click the Next button and then, if you want, edit the name for the shortcut in the Type a Name for This Shortcut text box. Wrap up by clicking Finish.

After you create a desktop shortcut, you can open the program, drive, folder, document, or Web page associated with it by double-clicking the shortcut icon or by right-clicking it and then choosing Open from its shortcut menu.

To change the size of all desktop icons, to disable the automatic arrangement of the icons and alignment to an invisible grid, or even to temporarily remove the display of all icons, right-click any open space on the desktop, choose View from the shortcut menu that appears, and then choose the appropriate option. To change the order in which your desktop shortcuts appear in columns across the desktop, use the options (Name, Size, Item Type, and Date Modified) on the Sort By shortcut menu, which you can access by right-clicking any open space on the desktop.

Flip and Flip 3-D

When you have many windows open in Windows 7, the Flip and Flip 3-D (also known as the Window Switcher) features provide you with two quick methods for activating the window you want to work by displaying it on the top of the others.

To use the Flip feature (see Figure 1-2), hold down Alt+Tab. Windows 7 displays a panel in the middle of the desktop showing thumbnails of each open window in the order in which they were opened with the name of the window that's currently selected. To activate a new window in the panel, press Tab as you hold down the Alt key until the thumbnail of that window is highlighted and its name appears. Then release the Alt key along with Tab to hide the panel display.

Figure 1-2

If you hold the Ctrl key down while you press the Alt and Tab key, Windows 7 opens a panel with thumbnails of all open windows, and this panel remains displayed even after you release these three keys. You can then flip through the panel by pressing the → or ← (to move forward or backward). When the thumbnail of the window you want to access is highlighted in the panel, press Enter to close the panel and display the selected window on the desktop.

To use the Flip 3D feature, hold down the Windows logo key (the key with picture of a waving flag divided into four parts,) and then press the Tab key. Windows 7 then displays all open windows in 3-D cascading arrangement (see Figure 1-3). You can then flip through the cascading thumbnails by continuing to the press the Tab key until the thumbnail of the window you want displayed is at the front of the stack. If your mouse has a center wheel, you can then flip through the 3-D stack by turning the wheel. (Turn the wheel forward to flip backward through the stack and backward to flip forward.)

As soon as you've brought the thumbnail of the window you want displayed on the desktop to the front of the 3-D stack, release the Windows logo key. Windows 7 then closes the cascading 3-D stack while at the same time displaying the selected window on the desktop.

If you hold the Ctrl key down while you press the Windows logo key and the Tab key, Windows 7 opens a 3-D stack of all open windows that remains displayed on your desktop even after you release these three keys. You can then flip through the 3-D stack by pressing the → or ← (to move forward and backward). When the thumbnail of the window you want to access is at the front of the stack, you can press Enter to close the stack and display its window on top of the desktop.

When all the open windows in Windows 7 are minimized as Quick Launch buttons (*see* "Taskbar" later in this part) on the taskbar — which happens after you click the Show the Desktop icon on the taskbar's shortcut menu or you press +D — remember that you can position the mouse pointer over each minimized button to display a thumbnail of its window. Then, when you see the image of the window you want to activate, you can position the mouse pointer on the thumbnail to temporarily display its window on the Windows 7 desktop either full screen or in its previous position and size. You can then click its Quick Launch button on the taskbar or displayed thumbnail to keep the window open on the desktop.

Figure 1-3

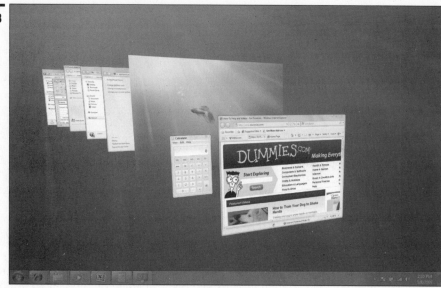

Gadgets

Gadgets are mini-applications (applets) for the Windows 7 desktop that give you access to frequently changing information, such as the current time, weather, stock quotes, news feeds, computer usage, and the like. Figure 1-4 shows you my desktop with the Gadgets Gallery window displayed. (*See* "Adding new gadgets to your desktop" later in this part.)

My desktop currently holds the following items:

- ✔ **Clock,** which shows an analog clock with the current time for any time zone you select.

- ✔ **Slide Show,** which displays a continuous slide show of the images that are stored in your Pictures library.

- ✔ **Calendar,** which shows the current day and date.

- ✔ **Weather,** which shows the current temperature (and when enlarged, weather conditions) for a selected town or city.

- ✔ **Feed Headlines,** which shows you news headlines for the RSS feed you select. (*See* "Internet Explorer 8" in Part 4 for details on RSS feeds and how to subscribe to them.)

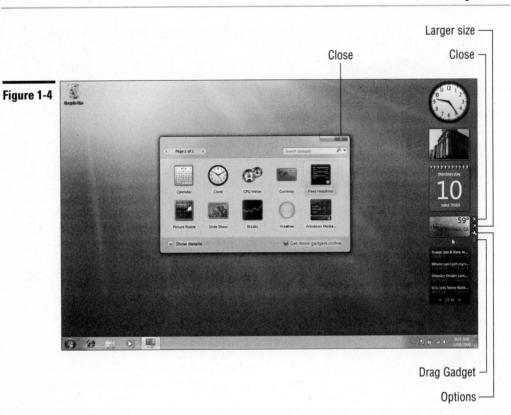

Figure 1-4

Larger size
Close
Close
Drag Gadget
Options

Adding new gadgets to your desktop

You can easily add gadgets to your Windows desktop. Not only can you select new gadgets from among those that are automatically shipped with the Windows 7 operating system, but you can always download gadgets from an ever-expanding online library. When you add new gadgets, Windows automatically displays them sequentially down a single column on the far right of your desktop (although, you can then move them anywhere you want on the desktop — *see* "Resizing gadgets and repositioning them on the desktop" later in this part).

To add gadgets to the desktop from among those that are included with Windows 7, follow these few steps:

1. Right-click the desktop and then choose Gadgets from the shortcut menu.

Windows 7 opens the Gadget Gallery window that displays all the gadgets on your computer, similar to the one shown in Figure 1-4.

2. Double-click the icon of the gadget you want to add to the desktop or right-click it and then click the Add option on the shortcut menu.

Windows adds the gadget to the right side of the Windows desktop.

3. When you finish adding gadgets, click the Close button in the Gadget Gallery window.

To download more gadgets from the Internet, open the Gadgets Gallery window as described in Step 1 and then click the Get More Gadgets Online link. Windows 7 then opens the Personalize Your PC Web page in the Internet Explorer. This page offers not only gadget news and instructions on how to download new gadgets, but also information on how to build your own gadgets, if you're so inclined.

To remove a gadget from the desktop, position the mouse pointer in the upper-right corner of the gadget you want to remove and then click the X that appears. Note that removing a gadget from the desktop doesn't delete it from your computer — to do that, you need to open the Gadgets Gallery window, right-click the gadget's thumbnail, and then choose Uninstall from its shortcut menu. To restore a gadget that you've removed from the desktop, just repeat the preceding steps for adding a new gadget.

Customizing the contents of a gadget

Many of the gadgets you add to the desktop are generic and need to be customized. For example, you can customize the Clock gadget by selecting a new clock face, giving it a name, and selecting a time zone other than your own. (By default, this analog clock automatically displays the same time as the digital time display in the notification area of the Windows 7 taskbar.) You also need to customize the Feed Headlines gadget so that it displays news headlines for a particular RSS feed to which you've subscribed. (*See* "Internet Explorer 8" in Part 4 for details on how to subscribe to an RSS feed.)

To customize the contents of a gadget, position the mouse pointer in the upper-right corner of the gadget and then click the wrench icon that appears immediately beneath the X. Alternatively, you can also right-click its icon and then choose Options from the shortcut menu. Windows 7 then opens a dialog box specific to the gadget that enables you to customize its display.

For example, if you open the settings dialog box for the Clock gadget (see Figure 1-5), you can then select a new clock face by clicking either the Next or Previous button (the ones with the triangles pointing right and left, respectively), and entering a clock name (such as London or Beijing) in the Clock Name text box. Next, select the appropriate time zone for the clock from the Time Zone drop-down list. In addition, this dialog box contains a Show the Second Hand check box that you can select if you want the Clock gadget to display a moving red second hand.

Figure 1-5

Changing the opacity of a gadget

In addition to customizing what information appears in a gadget (as in the RSS feed headlines shown in the Feed Headlines gadget), you can also customize the overall opacity of a gadget. Any gadget you add to the Windows 7 desktop is automatically displayed at 100-percent opacity (making it as opaque and non-see-through as possible). You can, however, lighten up any of your gadgets — making them more see-through — by changing the gadget's opacity.

To modify the opacity of a gadget, right-click the gadget and then highlight the Opacity item on its shortcut menu. Windows then displays a submenu where you can click the new opacity percentage item you want to use (20%, 40%, 60%, or 80%). The lower the percentage, the more transparent the gadget is.

Resizing gadgets and repositioning them on the desktop

Some gadgets have a Larger Size option that you can use to increase its display size on the desktop. To use this option, position the mouse pointer somewhere on the gadget and then click the Larger Size button (with an arrow pointing diagonally up to the right) that appears between the Close and Options buttons on the right size of the gadget (when the gadget offers this resizing option).

Immediately after you increase the display size of a gadget, the Larger Size button changes into a Smaller Size button that you can click whenever you want to return the gadget to its original display size on the desktop.

Windows 7 also enables you to reposition any gadget on the desktop by moving it out of its original position on the far right of the desktop. To relocate a gadget, position the mouse pointer on its Drag Gadget button (the one whose icon sports a grid of dots) that appears immediately beneath the Options button (the one with the wrench icon) on the right side of the gadget. Then, drag and drop the gadget in its new position on the Windows desktop just as you would any other desktop icon or the title bar of any open window.

Getting Started

The Windows 7 comes with a Getting Started window (shown in Figure 1-6), that you can open by clicking the Start button followed by the Getting Started option. The Getting Started window has links to an overview of the new Windows 7 operating system as well as help in dealing with common tasks associated with setting up your Windows 7 PC:

✔ **Discover Windows 7:** Opens the Windows 7 Home page on the Microsoft Web site in the Internet Explorer, where you can get the latest information about this latest and greatest version of the PC's favorite operating system.

✔ **Personalize Windows:** Enables you to select a new desktop background image, window colors, sounds, and screen saver as part of your personal Windows 7 settings. (*See* "Personalize" later in this part for details.)

✔ **Transfer Your Files:** Enables you to transfer your files, folders, e-mail, and other personal settings from another older computer running an earlier version of Windows to the current computer running Windows 7.

✔ **Share with a Homegroup:** Enables you to set up a new homegroup or join your computer to an existing one so that you can easily share files and resources such as printers and scanners. (*See* "Connect to a Network" in Part 3 for more on homegroups.)

✔ **Change UAC Settings:** Enables you to change the User Account Control settings that determine when you're notified about changes that programs are about to make to your computer. (*See* "Modifying User Account settings" in Part 5 for more.)

✔ **Get Windows Live Essentials:** Opens the Windows Live Essentials page in the Internet Explorer. On this page, you can get more information about the various Windows Live application programs, including Messenger, Mail, Writer, and Photo Gallery. The page also provides a convenient link for downloading the entire Live Essentials package.

✔ **Back Up Your Files:** Enables you to back up the files on your PC as well as restore files saved in a previous backup. (*See* "Backup and Restore" in Part 5 for details.)

✔ **Add New Users:** Enables you to make changes to your own user account as well as add new users to your computer. (*See* "Modifying User Account settings" in Part 5 for details.)

✔ **Change Text Size:** Enables you to increase the size of the text and icons displayed on the Windows 7 desktop.

To display information about the function of a particular option in the top section of the Getting Started window, click its icon and text description. To open the dialog box or window associated with a particular option, double-click its icon in the Getting Started window.

You can also access any of the options displayed in the Getting Started window directly from the Windows Start menu. Simply click Start and then position the mouse pointer on the Getting Started option (rather than clicking it) at the top of the Start menu. Windows then displays a submenu with each of the nine getting started options on it.

Figure 1-6

Help and Support

Windows 7 has an extensive help system that you can use not only to get general and detailed information on how to use Windows, but also to get answers from Microsoft on specific problems that you're experiencing. To open the Windows Help and Support window (see Figure 1-7), choose Start⇨Help and Support.

The Windows Help and Support window contains three main links in the Not Sure Where to Start section:

- ✔ **How to Get Started with Your Computer** displays a list of links to topics ranging from Protecting Your Computer to Installing Programs.

- ✔ **Learn About Windows Basics** displays a list of links to basic topics divided into the following six main categories: Learn about Your Computer;

Desktop Fundamentals; Programs, Files, and Folders; Internet, E-Mail, and Networking; Pictures and Games; and Help and Support.

✓ **Browse Help Topics** displays a Contents page with links to topics ranging from Getting Started to Hardware, Devices, and Drivers.

Figure 1-7

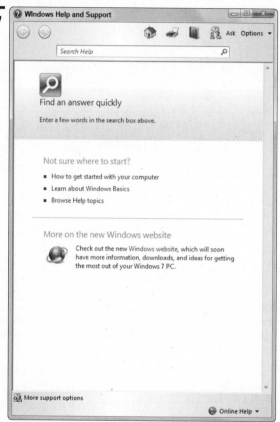

In addition to these links, the Windows Help and Support window contains a Search Help text box that you can use to search for particular topics. This text box works just like any other Search text box in Windows 7: Simply type the name of the feature you need help on (such as printing or searching files) and then click the Search Help button (the one with the magnifying glass icon) to display links to all related topics in the Windows Help and Support windoPersonalize

Windows 7 makes it easy for you to personalize your computer by selecting a new desktop background image, a color scheme for the various Windows elements, a screen saver to use when the computer has been idle for a certain period, as well as the sound effects to play when different events take place.

The easiest way to open the Personalization window (see Figure 1-8) for changing these settings is by right-clicking anywhere on the desktop background and then choosing Personalize at the bottom of the shortcut menu that appears.

Figure 1-8

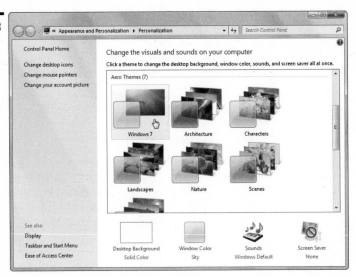

Note that you can also open this dialog box through the Control Panel (Start⇨Control Panel) by first clicking the Appearance and Personalization link followed by the Personalization link, but this method requires a whole lot more steps to do the same thing.

The options for customizing Windows 7 in the Personalization window include:

- ✔ **Change Desktop Icons:** Choosing this option opens the Desktop Icon Settings dialog box where you can specify which desktop icons to display on your desktop.

- ✔ **Change Mouse Pointers:** Clicking here opens the Mouse Properties dialog box with the Pointers tab selected, where you can select a new mouse pointer scheme — very helpful if you suffer a vision impairment that makes it difficult to track the normal mouse pointer — as well as customize what icons are used in various pointing situations.

- ✔ **Change Your Account Picture:** Using this option opens the Change Your Picture window, where you can select a new photo to represent you on the Windows 7 Start menu.

✔ **Display:** Click here to open the Display window, where you can adjust all sorts of display settings for the monitor or monitors connected to your computer, including the screen's brightness, text and icon size, screen resolution, and color depth. Note that the range of the resolution and color settings you have to choose from depends on the capabilities of your monitor or monitors.

✔ **Taskbar and Start Menu:** Click here to open the Taskbar and Start Menu Properties dialog box, where you can make changes to the appearance of the Windows taskbar, Start menu, and toolbars that appear on the taskbar. (*See* "Customizing the taskbar," "Customizing the Start menu," and "Adding other toolbars to the taskbar" later in this part for details.)

✔ **Ease of Access Center:** Use this option to open the Ease of Access Center window, where you can turn on and adjust a wide range of accessibility settings designed to make the personal computer easier to use for those with different visual and auditory physical impairments.

✔ **Change the Visuals and Sounds on Your Computer:** Use this pane of the Personalization window to select a new predefined theme for your Windows 7 desktop or to save the changes you've made to the desktop background, color scheme, sound effects, and screen saver (as described in the following bullets) as a new theme to reuse. To select a Windows XP color scheme, click Windows Classic or one of the high-contrast themes in the Basic and High Contrast area of the theme list box.

✔ **Desktop Background:** Click here to open the Desktop Background window (see Figure 1-9), where you can select new, ready-made wallpaper images, select your own photo images as the wallpaper (with the Browse button), change how the wallpaper image is displayed on the desktop (Fill, Fit, Stretch, Tile, or Center), or select a new solid color for the background by selecting Solid Colors from the Picture Location drop-down list.

✔ **Window Color:** Using this option opens the Window Color and Appearance window (see Figure 1-10), where you can select a new color and the amount of reflectiveness (called *glassiness* by Microsoft) for the title bars of windows, the Start menu, and taskbar.

✔ **Sounds:** Click here to open the Sounds tab in the Sound dialog box, where you can assign new sounds to different program events and save your new choices as a custom sound scheme to reuse.

✔ **Screen Saver:** Use this option to open the Screen Saver Settings dialog box, where you can select a new screen saver to use, customize the amount of idle time before the screen saver kicks in, and adjust your monitor and hard drive power settings (by clicking the Change Power Settings link).

Figure 1-9

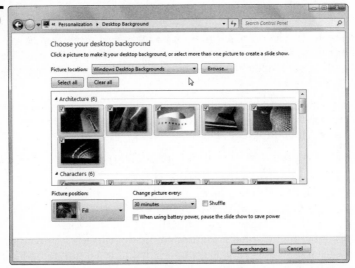

Figure 1-10

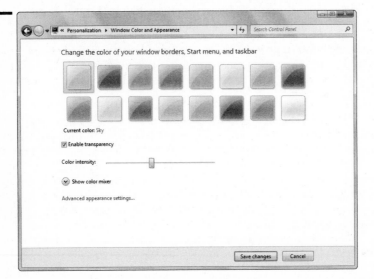

Taskbar

The taskbar is your almost constant companion in Windows 7. No matter where you go or what you do, the taskbar and the buttons of the various toolbars continue to be displayed along the bottom of the screen (unless you're using your computer to play a full-screen video or game). That way, you have access to all the neat features contained therein no matter whether you're writing a letter in your favorite word processor, surfing the Web with Internet Explorer 8, or perusing your favorite graphic images in the Windows Photo Viewer or Media Center.

The taskbar forms the base of the Windows desktop. Running along the bottom of the complete width of the screen, the Windows 7 taskbar, as shown in Figure 1-11, is divided into four sections:

- **The Start button,** with the accompanying Start menu at the far left.

- **Quick Launch buttons** for the Internet Explorer, Windows Explorer, and Media Player to the immediate right of the Start button. Click the Internet Explorer button to launch the Internet Explorer and display your Home page, click the Window Explorer button to open an Explorer window showing the Documents, Music, Picture, and Video libraries on your computer, and click the Media Player button to launch the Windows Media Player. (*See* "Windows Media Player" in Part 6.)

- **Buttons for open toolbars and minimized application windows** in the center area to the right of the Quick Launch buttons.

- **The notification area** (at the far right; sometimes called the system tray), with current time and icons showing the current status of computer components and programs as well as processes that are running in the background.

Whenever you minimize an open window by clicking its Minimize button in the upper-right corner, Windows 7 reduces the window to the appropriate Quick Launch or application button on the taskbar. Then, when you position the mouse pointer over a particular Quick Launch button, Windows displays thumbnail images of each of its open files above the button: Individual Web pages on different Web tabs are displayed above the Internet Explorer Quick Launch button, specific Windows 7 folders above the Windows Explorer button, the Media Player with playback controls above the Media Player button, and document files created with the particular program above the application buttons.

To display the document represented in a thumbnail, position the mouse pointer somewhere on the thumbnail image. To then reopen the document on the Windows desktop, simply click the thumbnail image.

**Figure
1-11**

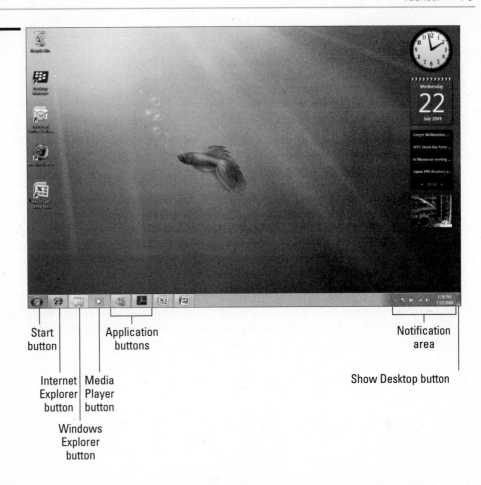

Start
button

Application
buttons

Notification
area

Internet | Media
Explorer | Player
button | button

Show Desktop button

Windows
Explorer
button

TIP

To minimize all open windows and clear the desktop, click the Show Desktop
button (the rectangle at the very end of the taskbar, to the immediate right of
the notification area), press +D or right-click the taskbar and then choose
Show the Desktop from the shortcut menu that appears. To once redisplay all
the open windows on the desktop in their original order, click the Show Desktop
button or press +D again or right-click the taskbar and this time, click Show
Open Windows on its shortcut menu. To temporarily hide the contents of all
open windows displaying only their outlines on the desktop with the new Aero
Peek feature, simply position the mouse pointer on the Show Desktop button
instead of clicking it.

Remember that when you have multiple windows open at the same time on the desktop, you can use the Flip or Flip 3-D feature to bring a particular window to the top of the stack. (*See* "Flip and Flip 3-D" earlier in this part.)

The Start menu

The Start button that opens the Start menu (see Figure 1-12) always appears as the first button on the taskbar. The Start menu is the most basic menu in Windows, giving you access to all the stuff on your computer.

To open the Start menu, simply click the Start button icon in the lower-left corner of the taskbar, press the   button, or press Ctrl+Esc on your keyboard.

The Start menu is divided into two columns. The options in the right column of the Start menu are fixed and never change. (Note that your user picture and name are included as part of these fixed items, appearing at the top of the right column.) As for the left column, only the All Programs button, the Search Programs and Files text button (at the bottom), and the Internet Explorer options (at the top) are fixed. The other icons that appear in this column change over time to represent the applications that you launch most frequently.

To ensure that a particular item remains on the Start menu, open the menu, right-click the item you want added, and then choose Pin to Start Menu from its shortcut menu.

**Figure
1-12**

To run one of the recently used programs, simply click that icon in the left column of the Start menu. To open a Windows Explorer window for a particular Windows component — Documents, for example, or Computer, or Network, or Control Panel — click the component's button in the right column of the Start menu.

To launch an application program or open a Windows Explorer window or the Control Panel that does not appear on the Start menu, type the first few characters of its name in the Search Programs and Files text box and then click the link for the sought-for program that appears in the Search Results on the Start menu to launch or open it.

To display a list of all the application programs installed on your computer, click the All Programs option on the Start menu. You can then launch the application by clicking its folder (if the program uses one) and then clicking its program icon and name on the Start menu.

To shut down your computer at the end of the workday, press your computer's Power button or click the Shut Down button that appears to the immediate right of the Search Programs and Files button. Windows then prompts you to save any unsaved changes before closing down open application programs, logging you off, and powering down your system. (*See* "Restart, Sleep/Hibernate, Lock, Log Off, and Shut Down" in Part 2 for details about the other Power button options.)

See "Customizing the Start menu" later in this part for details on how you can change the look and contents of the Start menu.

Customizing the taskbar

The Taskbar and Start Menu Properties dialog box enables you to customize the settings for the taskbar and the Start menu. To open this dialog box, right-click the Start button or any open area (with no buttons) on the taskbar and then choose Properties from the shortcut menu that appears. After the dialog box makes its appearance, click the Taskbar tab. (See Figure 1-13.)

The options in the Taskbar Appearance section at the top of the Taskbar tab do the following:

- **Lock the Taskbar:** Locks all the bars so that you can't adjust the size of the different toolbar areas of the taskbar.

- **Auto-Hide the Taskbar:** Hides the taskbar until you roll the mouse pointer somewhere over that position. This way, the taskbar appears only when you need it.

- **Use Small Icons:** Reduces the height of the taskbar and accordingly the size of all the buttons and toolbars displayed on it.

✔ **Taskbar Location on Screen:** Enables you to select the position of the taskbar — Bottom (the default), Left, Right, or Top.

✔ **Taskbar Buttons:** Enables you to determine how the buttons for minimized documents open in the various Windows components and applications are displayed and whether or not they're combined so that one type of Quick Launch button appears (with individual thumbnails above) or each appears in individual buttons on the taskbar. Your options here are Always Combine, Hide Labels (the default), Combine When Taskbar Is Full, or Never Combine.

Figure 1-13

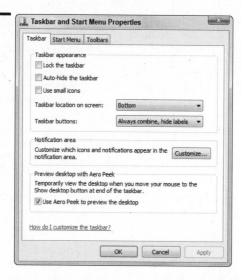

Near the bottom of the Taskbar tab, you can find the Use Aero Peek to Preview the Desktop check box. When this check box is selected (as it is by default), keep in mind that you can temporarily hide all but the outlines of the windows that are currently open on the Windows desktop simply by positioning the mouse pointer over the Show Desktop button located at the far-right end of the taskbar. The contents of the open windows are then instantly redisplayed on the desktop the moment you move the mouse pointer off of the Show Desktop button.

See "Customizing the Notification area," later in this part, for information about using the Customize button under Notification Area on the Taskbar tab of the Taskbar and Start Menu Properties dialog box to modify the appearance of this part of the Windows taskbar.

Customizing the Start menu

To customize the appearance of the Start menu, you need to click the Start Menu tab in the Taskbar and Start Menu Properties dialog box. To modify what items automatically appear on the Start menu and how they're displayed, you then click the Customize button to open the Customize Start Menu dialog box. (See Figure 1-14.)

Use the check boxes in the list box of the Customize Start Menu dialog box to control which items appear on the Start menu. For example, to add a Network item that opens the Network window (where you can see all the devices connected on your network), select the Network check box. Likewise, to remove the Default Programs item that opens the Default Programs dialog box (where you can configure what default programs to use for tasks such as Web browsing and reading e-mail), deselect the Default Programs check box.

To change the way fixed icons, such as Computer, Control Panel, Documents, and the like, are displayed in the right-hand column of the Start menu, click one of the following option buttons under Computer at the top of the Customize Start Menu dialog box:

> ✔ **Display As a Link:** This option is the default setting for all fixed items. It causes Windows to open a separate folder window showing the item folders and files.

Figure 1-14

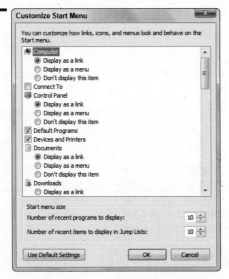

✔ **Display As a Menu:** Select this option when you want Windows 7 to display the item folders and files as menu items on a continuation menu that you can select and open from the Start menu.

✔ **Don't Display This Item:** Select this option to remove the display of the fixed item, such as Network Places.

After changing items in the Customize Start Menu dialog box, click its OK button and then click the Apply button on the Start Menu tab in the Taskbar and Start Menu Properties dialog box. This enables you to open the Start menu to check that the modifications you want on the Start menu have been put into place before you click OK in the Taskbar and Start Menu Properties dialog box to close it.

Beneath the Customize button on the Start Menu tab of the Taskbar and Start Menu Properties dialog box, you find a Power Button Action drop-down list. You can use this drop-down list to change the function of the button that appears to the immediate right of the Search Programs and Files button at the bottom of the Start menu from Shut Down to any of the other options found on the associated pop-up menu (Switch User, Log Off, Lock, Restart, Sleep, or Hibernate). After you select a new function for the Power Button, the name of its option appears on the button, and the previously defined function then appears on the associated pop-up menu.

If you don't want Windows 7 to add the names of the programs you recently worked in or the names of files you recently opened to the Start menu, you can prevent this addition. Simply deselect the Store and Display Recently Opened Programs in the Start Menu check box and the Store and Display Recently Opened Items in the Start Menu and the Taskbar check box, which appear at the bottom of the Start Menu tab in the Taskbar and Start Menu Properties dialog box.

The Windows 7 Start menu adds jump lists to the application icons (such as Microsoft Office Word or Excel) that appear on it. Jump lists show the documents you recently opened with the particular program, and you can use their items to quickly launch the application while at the same time reopening the document for more editing. If you have a document that you regularly edit, you can even pin it to the program's jump list by clicking the Pin to This List button that appears when you position the mouse pointer over the document's filename. That way, the document doesn't disappear from the program's jump list as you continue editing other files with the program.

Pinning icons to the taskbar

The Windows 7 taskbar contains three standard Quick Launch buttons that you can use to start commonly used programs:

✔ **Internet Explorer:** Opens Internet Explorer 8 for browsing Web pages. (*See* "Internet Explorer 8" in Part 4.)

✔ **Windows Explorer:** Opens the Libraries window in the Windows Explorer so that you can access documents stored on your computer. (**See** "File, Folder, and Library Management" in Part 2.)

✔ **Windows Media Player:** Opens Windows Media Player so that you can view photos or play music or video stored on your computer. (**See** "Windows Media Player" in Part 6.)

In addition to these three standard Quick Launch buttons, you can add your own custom buttons by dragging a desktop shortcut to the desired position on the taskbar and then releasing the mouse button when the Pin to Taskbar ScreenTip appears above the shortcut icon. The mouse pointer indicates where the new button will be inserted with a dark I-beam cursor at the tip of the pointer. A button for the shortcut then appears at the position of the I-beam on the taskbar.

You can delete any of these custom Quick Launch buttons from the taskbar by right-clicking the button and then choosing Unpin from Taskbar from the shortcut menu that appears.

As you continue to add new Quick Launch buttons to the taskbar, some of the existing buttons at the end of the bar become hidden from view when the Lock the Taskbar option is selected (as it is by default). Windows 7 then adds a continuation button with triangles pointing up and down to the taskbar. Click the triangle pointing downward on this continuation button to display hidden buttons at the end of the taskbar, and click the triangle pointing upward to redisplay the buttons at the beginning of the taskbar.

Adding other toolbars to the taskbar

When you first start using Windows 7, none of its built-in toolbars are added to the taskbar. You can, however, add any of the following toolbars:

✔ **Address toolbar:** Here you can directly enter pathnames for folders and files you want to open or URL addresses for Web pages you want to visit.

✔ **Links toolbar:** Enables you to add links to Web pages you visit regularly by dragging the Web page icon — located to the immediate left of the page's URL address — to a place on the toolbar.

✔ **Tablet PC Input Panel toolbar:** This toolbar (a button, actually) opens the Input Panel on the Windows 7 desktop where you can write rather than type your entries (assuming that you're running Windows 7 on a Tablet PC laptop computer).

✔ **Desktop toolbar:** Gives you access to all the desktop items on your computer.

To add any (or all) of these toolbars to your taskbar, right-click the bar at a place where there isn't already a toolbar and then choose Toolbars from the pop-up menu that appears, followed by the name of the toolbar to add.

Creating new toolbars

You can add your own custom toolbars to the Windows 7 taskbar from the folders that you keep on your computer. When you create a custom toolbar from an existing folder, Windows creates buttons for each of the subfolders that the folder may contain.

To create a custom toolbar from a folder, follow these steps:

1. Right-click the taskbar (without clicking any of the buttons or icons it contains) and then choose Toolbars⇨New Toolbar from the shortcut menu that appears.

Windows opens the New Toolbar – Choose a Folder dialog box, where you select the folder to be used in creating the new toolbar.

2. Use the Navigation pane in the Choose a Folder dialog box to select the folder whose contents are to be used in creating the new toolbar by clicking the folder icon in the navigation list box.

3. Click the OK button to close the New Toolbar dialog box.

As soon as you close the New Toolbar dialog box, Windows adds the new toolbar, indicated by the folder's name followed by a continuation button (>>). When you click this continuation button, Windows 7 displays a pop-up menu showing all the subfolders and documents contained in that folder.

 All custom toolbars that you create are automatically deleted the moment you remove their display from the Windows 7 taskbar (by right-clicking the taskbar and then choosing Toolbars followed by the name of the custom toolbar).

The notification area

The notification area displays the current time as well as icons that indicate the active status of various components — the status of your network connection, Active Sync connection to your hand-held device, hot-pluggable cards such as PC cards or ExpressCards inserted into a laptop computer, or the printer queue, to name a few examples. In addition, the notification area displays icons representing various programs or processes that run in the background, such as the Windows Sidebar (for hiding and redisplaying the Sidebar), the Language Bar (for using Voice Recognition and Handwriting Recognition in Microsoft Office programs), the Windows Clipboard when it contains multiple items, and Windows Messenger.

This is also the place from which the Windows Update feature displays its Update Reminder message telling you that new updates for the system are available. (*See* "Windows Update" in Part 5.)

To identify an icon that appears in the status area, position the mouse pointer over it until the ScreenTip appears. To change the status of an icon, right-click it to display the pop-up menu and then click the appropriate menu option. For example, to open the Volume Control dialog box to adjust the volume of your speakers, right-click the speaker icon in the notification area and then choose Open Volume Mixer from the pop-up menu that appears.

 To temporarily expand the notification area so that all of its icons are displayed, click the Show Hidden Icons button (the one to the left of the first displayed icon in this area, sporting a triangle pointing upward). Note that you can also customize the notification area as part of customizing the taskbar and Start menu properties. (*See* the next section, "Customizing the notification area," for more information.)

Customizing the notification area

You can also customize the settings for the notification area of the taskbar by altering the settings in the Notification Area Icons window opened by clicking the Customize button in the Notification Area of the Taskbar tab in the Taskbar and Start Menu Properties dialog box, which in turn is opened by right-clicking the taskbar and then choosing Properties from the shortcut menu that appears.

In the Notification Area Icons window, you can change the circumstances under which particular notification icons are displayed in the notification area and also turn the display of system icons on and off.

The list box in this window is divided into two columns: Icons and Behaviors. You can then change the way a particular icon is displayed in the notification area by selecting any of the following behaviors on its Behaviors drop-down button:

- ✔ **Show Icon and Notification:** Displays the particular process's icon in your notification area as well as any notifications above the icon.

- ✔ **Hide Icon and Notification:** Displays neither the process's icon nor notification in your notification area.

- ✔ **Only Show Notifications:** Displays a process's notification above the notification area without also displaying its icon.

 If you want all icons on your notification area displayed along with their notifications, you can turn on the Show Icon and Notification setting for all the icons in one step: Simply click the Always Show All Icons and Notifications on the Taskbar check box at the bottom of the Notification Area Icons window and then click OK.

Arranging windows on the desktop

Normally when you open multiple windows on the desktop, they overlap one another, with only the most recently opened window fully displayed on top. As you open more windows, it becomes increasingly difficult to arrange them so that the information you need is displayed onscreen. (The arrangement is especially difficult to manage when copying or moving files and folders between open windows.)

To help you organize the windows you have open, Windows 7 offers several arrangement options. To rearrange the open windows with one of these options, right-click the taskbar at a place that isn't occupied by a window button and then choose one of the following options from the shortcut menu that appears:

- ✔ **Cascade Windows** to overlap the open windows so that the title bars are all displayed one above the other in a cascade

- ✔ **Show Windows Stacked** to place the windows vertically one on top of the other

- ✔ **Show Windows Side by Side** to place the windows horizontally side by side

- ✔ **Show the Desktop** to reduce all the windows open on the desktop to minimized buttons on the taskbar

 In Windows 7, you can now resize windows open on the desktop simply by dragging them to particular positions on the screen. To maximize a window on the desktop, drag it to the very top of the screen. To get a particular window ready to be displayed side by side, drag it to the left or right edge of the screen until its window is resized to fit half the screen. Then, repeat this resizing process with the second window using the opposite side of the screen.

Using the Task Manager

Windows Task Manager keeps tabs on your system and how it's running. You can use Task Manager to get an overview of what programs and processes are running on your computer. You can also use it to switch to programs and to end programs that have stopped responding (in other words, programs that have frozen up on you).

To open Windows Task Manager, right-click the taskbar at a place where there are no buttons and then choose Start Task Manager from the shortcut menu that appears. Figure 1-15 shows you Windows Task Manager when running three different applications.

To switch to another program or window from Windows Task Manager, click it in the list box on the Applications tab and then click the Switch To button. Windows then minimizes Task Manager and displays the selected window on the desktop.

Figure 1-15

To end a process or program that has frozen up on you, click it in the list box on the Applications tab and then click the End Task command button. Note that you'll probably get an alert dialog box indicating that the program has stopped responding. Click the End command button in this dialog box (as many times as you have to) to get Windows 7 to kill the process.

The status bar of Windows Task Manager shows you statistics on the number of processes running under the program, the percentage of the CPU (Central Processing Unit, the big chip at the heart of the computer), and the memory usage of the program. If you like to look at schematics, click the Performance tab in this window to see a dynamic charting of the total CPU and memory usage on your computer (and to find really useful stuff like the number of handles, threads, and processes that are being run).

Computer Management

Computer processing isn't really much more than managing the application programs and data files on your computer. To effectively manage Windows 7, you also need to know about the physical media on which they're stored (hard drives, CD-ROMs, and the like) as well as the structure of the folders in which they're arranged. In this part, you get the lowdown on disk, file, folder, library, and program management. For good measure, I throw in info on how to use Windows Explorer to keep tabs on this stuff.

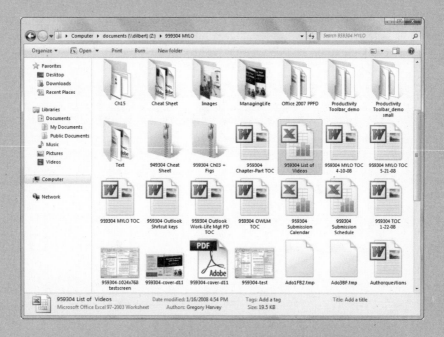

In this part . . .

- ✔ **Accessing Hard Drives and All Kinds of Removable Media**
- ✔ **Creating New Files, Folders, and Libraries**
- ✔ **Copying and Moving Files and Folders**
- ✔ **Deleting Files and Folders**
- ✔ **Navigating Your Computer with Windows Explorer**

Disk Management

In Windows 7, the Computer window (Start⇨Computer) is the place to go when you need access or information about all the drives (including non-physical — or virtual — drives mapped to network folders) and disks connected to your computer system.

Figure 2-1 shows the Computer window for my laptop computer running Windows 7. As you can see, Windows 7 automatically separates the various drive icons into the following three categories:

🖝 **Hard Disk Drives,** of which there is one: SQ00483V02 (C:)

🖝 **Devices with Removable Storage,** of which there is one connected to the computer: DVD-RW Drive (D:)

🖝 **Network Location,** which contains a single network drive named Documents on Dilbert, mapped to the Z: drive

Figure 2-1

 TIP

The Preview pane at the bottom of the Computer window gives you valuable statistics about any drive that you select, including the total size, the amount of free space (which is also shown visually in the Space Used indicator), and the type of file system (the older FAT32 supported by Windows 95, 98, and Me or the newer NTFS also supported by Windows XP, 2000, and Vista).

Opening folders on drives in the Computer window

To open any of the drives or disks that appear in your Computer window so you can display the folders and files they contain, double-click its drive icon in the central area of the Computer window or right-click it and then click Open. (If you want to see the contents of the drive in a separate Explorer window, click Open in New Window instead.)

To collapse a category in the Computer window to temporarily hide its drive icons, click the collapse button (the one with the black triangle pointing downward before the category name). To later expand a collapsed category to once again display its hidden drive icons, click the expand button for the hidden category. (The expand button automatically replaces the collapse button and points directly at the category name.)

Formatting a disk

In this day and age, when floppy disk drives are almost never included in new computer systems, you might never experience the "joy" of formatting a floppy disk. Almost all the disks that you purchase today, including CDs and DVDs, come preformatted. (The formatting is done as part of the automated process that checks the disks for errors.) From time to time, you may want to reformat a prepared disk — especially a flash drive that you connect to your computer via one of its USB ports — that has become corrupted or that contains data that you no longer need. In very rare situations, heaven forbid, you may even have to reformat a hard drive on your computer.

To format a disk or computer drive, follow these steps:

1. When formatting a floppy, CD, or DVD, insert the blank disk or a disk that holds files and folders that you don't give a hoot about.

2. Open the Computer window (Start⇨Computer) and then right-click the icon of the drive that holds the disk (or that you want to reformat).

3. Choose the Format command from the shortcut menu that appears to open the Format dialog box.

   To format any hard drive on your computer, your user account must be an administrator type. You cannot, however, reformat the drive that contains the Windows 7 operating system (unless you're reinstalling Windows using the Windows 7 Install disc).

4. (Optional) Select the Capacity for the size of the disk that you're formatting.

   When formatting a floppy disk, choose the lesser (double-density) capacity 3.5", 720KB, 512 bytes/sector if you inserted that kind of disk into your floppy drive.

5. (Optional) By default, Windows XP selects NTFS (supported by Windows XP, 2000, Vista, and 7) in the File System drop-down list box as the file system for which to format the disk. If you're formatting a floppy disk for an older system running Windows 95, 98, or Me, select FAT on the File System drop-down list.

6. (Optional) Type a label in the Volume Label text box if you want to attach a name to the floppy, CD, DVD, or flash drive that you can use to identify it. When you format by using the FAT system, you're restricted to 11 characters; when you're using the NTFS system, you're limited to a maximum of 32 characters.

7. (Optional) Click the Quick Format check box in the Format Options (if you're reformatting a disk that contains files and folders that you no longer need). If you're formatting a brand-new disk, leave this check box empty.

8. (Optional) If you're formatting a floppy or CD as a startup disk for a MS-DOS computer, click the Create an MS-DOS Startup Disk check box.

9. Click the Start button to begin formatting the disk and then click OK in the alert dialog box warning you that formatting erases all data currently on the disk.

After you click Start and then OK, Windows keeps you informed of the progress in the Formatting box at the bottom of the Format dialog box. If you need to stop the process before it's complete, click the Cancel button.

Mapping a network folder as a local drive

If your computer is part of a local area network and you use files that are stored in folders on another networked computer, you will find it helpful to map a drive letter to that network folder so that you can access it directly from the Computer window. When you *map* a drive, Windows lists the network folder as a drive in the Network Location section of various Internet Explorer windows (such as Computer, Documents, and so on) as well as in the Computer section of the Navigation pane of various application program's Open dialog boxes (Word, Excel, and so forth). This setup makes it very quick and easy to locate the folder and access its various files (especially if you set it up so that Windows automatically maps the drive each time you start the computer).

To be able to map a network folder to a local drive, the folder must be shared and you must have network permission to access it on the other computer.

To map a network folder to a drive letter on your computer, follow these steps:

1. Open the Computer window by choosing Start⇨Computer.

2. Click the Map Network Drive button on the toolbar to open the Map Network Drive dialog box. (See Figure 2-2.)

3. Select an unused drive letter for the network folder in the Drive drop-down list.

Figure 2-2

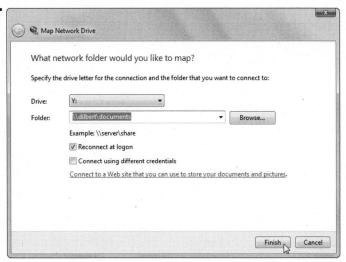

4. In the Folder text box, enter the network share pathname (following the `\\server\share` example shown beneath the Folder text box), either by clicking the drop-down button to the immediate right of the text box and selecting its previously entered pathname from the list, or by clicking the Browse button and locating the shared network folder in the Browse For Folder dialog box. When you're done, click OK.

5. (Optional) If you want Windows to re-create this network drive by mapping the network folder to the same drive letter each time you start the computer, select the Reconnect at Logon check box. Also, if you don't have permission to create the network (as an administrator), select the Connect Using Different Credentials check box and then enter the username and password of one of the administrators on your network (assuming you know his username and have access to his password) in the Windows Security dialog box that appears before you click OK.

6. Click the Finish button.

When you click Finish, Windows creates the network drive and automatically opens it in Windows Explorer. After that, you can access any of the folder's subfolders and files by simply opening the network drive in the Computer window.

Note that Windows 7 indicates a mapped network drive by automatically assigning it to the Network Location category in the Computer window.

File, Folder, and Library Management

Files contain all the precious data that you create with those sophisticated Windows-based programs. Files occupy a certain amount of space rated either in kilobytes (KB, or thousands of bytes) or megabytes (MB, or millions of bytes) on a particular disk, be it your hard drive, a CD-ROM, a DVD, or even, in very rare cases, a removable floppy disk.

Folders are the data containers in Windows 7. They can contain files, other folders, or a combination of files and folders. Like files, folders occupy a certain amount of space (rated in KB or MB) on the particular drive.

Libraries are the larger containers that enable you to group all the folders and files of a particular type. When you begin using Windows 7, you have four libraries that you can use: Documents (for all text documents), Music (for your tunes), Pictures (for all photos and other graphic files), and Videos (for your movies). You can then create other libraries as you need them as well as add files and folders to each of these predefined libraries.

As you open folders and subfolders to get to the file you want to use in one of the Explorer windows, Windows keeps track of the path in the address bar at the top of the window. This path starts with the disk or folder icon followed by the names of drives, folders, and subfolders in succession separated by a triangle pointing to the right (indicating a new sublevel).

For example, the address bar at the top of the Computer window shown in Figure 2-3 shows you the path for finding an Excel worksheet file named Invoice 021509. The file is stored in a Payables subfolder within an Accounts folder on my computer's local hard drive (C:).

If you click the drop-down button at the right end of the address bar (or anywhere inside the address bar but outside of the path itself), Windows 7 converts the path in the address bar into the more traditional form of a pathname separated by backslashes that's used exclusively in the previous versions of Windows. For example, after clicking the address bar's drop-down button in the Computer window shown in Figure 2-3, its path immediately changed to

```
C:\Accounts\Payables\
```

This more traditional pathname format is what you see when you open a drop-down menu in an address bar in an Explorer window or the Address toolbar on the taskbar. (*See* "Adding other toolbars to the taskbar" in Part 1.) When specifying the pathname for a file by using this format, you simply append the filename to the path, as in

```
C:\Accounts\Payables\Invoice 021509
```

Figure 2-3

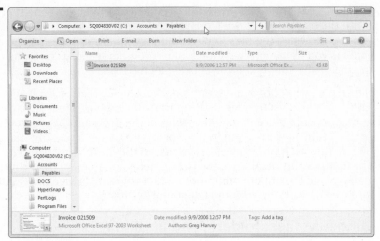

The Navigation pane that appears in the left column of an Explorer window enables you to open the folders and subfolders containing the folder with the files you want to work with in Windows. As you double-click a folder icon in the Navigation pane, Windows 7 adds its name to the Explorer window's address bar. Then, to open one of the files displayed in the Explorer window, select the file in the main part of the window and click the Open button on the taskbar or right-click the file's icon and choose Open from its shortcut menu. Keep in mind that a file's shortcut menu also contains many other options for working with the file. The options include: Print, Open With, Cut, Copy, Send To, Delete, Rename, and Properties, to name the ones you'll most commonly use.

Assigning filenames

Each filename in Windows 7 consists of two parts: a main filename and a file extension. The file extension, which identifies the type of file and what program created it, is traditionally three characters, although extensions for newer apps such as Microsoft Office Word 2007 (.docx) and Excel 2007 (.xlsx), as well as .html for Web pages, are four characters. File extensions are automatically assigned by the creating agent or program, and Windows 7 doesn't normally display extensions as part of filenames that appear in Windows Explorer. For information on how to display file extensions as part of the filename, *see* "Customizing a window's folder options" later in this part.

Whereas the creating program normally assigns the file extension, Windows 7 enables you to call the main part of the filename whatever the heck you want, up to a maximum of 255 characters (including spaces!). Keep in mind, however, that all pre-Windows 95 programs, and even some that run on Windows 98, don't support long filenames. These programs allow a maximum of only eight characters, with no spaces.

In Windows 7, files are assigned distinctive file icons indicating the type of file along with the filenames. These icons help you quickly identify the type of file when you're browsing the files in your folders with Windows Explorer. An icon also enables you to launch the appropriate program while at the same time opening the file by simply double-clicking its file icon.

You can change what program opens a particular file. Right-click its file icon and then choose Properties to open its Properties dialog box. Then click the Change button that appears to the immediate right of the program that currently opens the file. Select the new program in the Open With dialog box. Note that if you can't locate the program you want to assign to the file in the Open With list box, click the Browse button and use the Navigation pane to open the Program Files folder and locate the application there. (*See* "Program Management" later in this part for more on working with the Program Files folder.)

Creating new files, folders, and libraries

You can create new files to hold new data and new folders to hold your files right within Windows 7.

To create a new, empty folder, follow these steps:

1. Open the Windows Explorer window (such as Documents or Computer) in which the new folder is to appear.

2. Click the New Folder button on the window's toolbar.

   If the Classic menus are displayed along the top of the Explorer window immediately above the taskbar, you can also choose File⇨New⇨Folder or, if not, press Alt+FWF.

3. Replace the temporary folder name (New Folder) by first typing a name of your choosing and then pressing Enter.

To create an empty file that holds a certain type of information, follow these steps:

1. Open the Windows Explorer window where the new file is required.

2. Right-click a blank area in the window's display area and then choose New from the shortcut menu that appears.

   If the Classic menus are displayed in the Explorer window, you can also choose File⇨New from the menu bar; if not, press Alt+FW.

3. Choose the type of file you want to create (such as Microsoft Office Word Document, Microsoft Office Excel Worksheet, Text Document, Briefcase, and so on) from the New submenu.

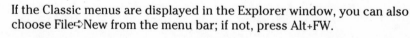

4. Replace the temporary filename (such as New Microsoft Word Document) by typing a name of your choosing and pressing Enter.

Create a new folder when you need to have a new place to store your files and other folders. If you want to, you can even create an empty file in a particular folder before you actually put something in the file — remember that you can always launch the associated program and open the blank file in it by double-clicking its file icon.

Create a new library when you need to have a place to store all the folders and files that fall into a particular category. For example, if your company deals with a lot of different forms, you might want to create a Forms library where you store all the various form document files, each within its own folder. To create a new library devoted to forms, you'd open the Documents window (Start⇨Documents) and then right-click the Libraries icon in the Navigation pane and click New⇨Library on its shortcut menu. Windows 7 then adds a New Library to the list of existing libraries that you can then rename Forms.

Customizing a window's folder options

Windows 7 enables you to customize many aspects of a folder's appearance and behavior in an open window by using the controls in the Folder Options dialog box. (See Figure 2-4.) To open this dialog box, click the Organize button (the first button on a window's toolbar) and then choose Folder and Search Options from its drop-down menu.

If the Classic menus are displayed in the Explorer window, you can also open the Folder Options dialog box by choosing Tools⇨Folder Options. If they aren't displayed, press Alt+TO.

The Folder Options dialog box contains three tabs:

- ✔ **General** controls whether Explorer windows open in the same or a new window, as well as how you select items in an open window and how you select and open folders and files. It also contains Navigation pane options that determine whether or subfolders are automatically displayed in the pane (Show All Folders) or whether they automatically expand to show the folders above the one currently selected in the pane (Automatically Expand to Current Folder).

- ✔ **View** controls how files and folders appear in an open window.

- ✔ **Search** controls how searches are conducted in Explorer windows and whether the searches use non-indexed locations for searching the contents of files (which makes them very much faster to find) or just their filenames.

Figure 2-4

Changing how you select and open items

Normally, you click to select an item in an open window (indicated by highlighting its name and/or icon) and double-click to open the item. If you're more of the Web-surfing type, you can change this scheme by selecting the Single-Click to Open an Item (Point to Select) option on the General tab of the Folder Options dialog box. After selecting this option, you only have to point to an item in a folder and click it once to open it.

TIP

When you choose the Single-Click to Open an Item (Point to Select) option on the General tab, Windows 7 automatically activates and selects the Underline Icon Titles Only When I Point at Them option as well. When this option is in effect, you see the underlining (akin to a hyperlink on a Web page) only when you actually position the mouse pointer over the item. If you want this hyperlink-type underlining to always appear beneath items you open in a window (making windows even more like your typical Web page), select the Underline Icon Titles Consistent with My Browser option instead.

Changing how items are displayed in a folder

The View tab of the Folder Options dialog box (see Figure 2-5) contains a wide variety of options for controlling the appearance of the items in the Explorer windows you open. Among the most important options on this tab, you find the following:

- ✓ **Always Show Menus:** Select this check box to ensure that each window displays the good old menus, File through Help, above the taskbar in the Explorer window (not selected by default). That way, you always have access to these tried-and-true menus without having to remember to press the Alt key!

✔ **Display the Full Path in the Title Bar (Classic Theme Only):** Enable this option to have Windows 7 display the folder's traditional pathname (with the drive letter separated by the different folders and subfolders separated by backslashes) in the Explorer window's title bar, assuming that your computer employs one of the Classic desktop themes to make your copy of Windows 7 more like the Windows 95 and 98 you once knew and loved. (*See* "Personalize" in Part 1 for details.)

✔ **Hidden Files and Folders:** This particular option comes with its own two (sub)options: Do Not Show Hidden Files, Folders, or Drives (selected by default) to hide the display of certain system-type files and folders, and Show Hidden Files, Folders, and Drives to display them.

✔ **Hide Extensions for Known File Types:** Select this check box (not selected by default) to suppress the display of the filename extensions such as .doc, .xlsx, and .html.

To apply all the changes you make on the View tab for the currently selected Explorer folder to all the Explorer windows in Windows 7 (Documents, Computer, and so forth), finish making your changes and then be sure you click the Apply to Folders button at the top of the View tab in the Folder Options dialog box before you click the OK button. Click the Restore Defaults button at the bottom of the View tab of the Folder Options dialog box whenever you want to restore all the Windows 7 original view settings.

Figure 2-5

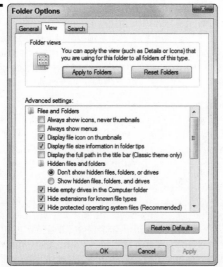

Creating compressed (zipped) folders

If you're running short on hard drive space, you can conserve precious free space by creating compressed folders that automatically compress every file and subfolder that you put into them. To create a blank compressed folder, follow these steps:

1. In Windows Explorer, navigate to where you want the new compressed folder to be.

2. Right-click in a blank area anywhere in the central part of the window's display area and then choose New from the shortcut menu that appears. Click Compressed (Zipped) Folder on its continuation menu.

   If the Classic menus are displayed in the Explorer window, you can also choose File⇨New⇨Compressed (Zipped) Folder. If not, press Alt+FW and then click Compressed (Zipped) folder on the continuation menu.

   Windows creates a new folder icon (sporting a zipper to indicate its special zip-type compression abilities) that sports the temporary filename New Compressed (Zipped) Folder.

3. Replace the temporary filename, New Compressed (Zipped) Folder, by typing your own filename; press Enter.

After creating a compressed folder, you can copy or move files and folders into it just as you would a regular file folder. As you copy or move files or folders, Windows 7 compresses their contents. You can then copy compressed folders to removable media, such as CD-ROMs and flash drives. You can also attach them to e-mail messages.

Microsoft has even gone so far as to make its compression schemes compatible with other compression programs. This compatibility means that you can send compressed folders to people who don't even use Windows (if you know any), and they can extract (decompress) their contents by using their favorite compression/decompression program.

Note that Windows 7 automatically appends the .zip file extension to the name you give a compressed folder as a way to identify the folder as one containing zipped-up files. Of course, you must make sure the Hide Extensions For Known File Types check box on the View tab of the Folder Options dialog box is deselected in order for this filename extension to be displayed in Windows Explorer.

You can run program files from within compressed folders simply by double-clicking their program icons, provided that the program doesn't depend upon any other files (such as those pesky .dll files or some sort of data files). If the programs in the compressed folder do depend upon these kinds of auxiliary files, you must extract them before you can run the program. Also, be aware that when you open text or graphic documents stored in a compressed folder, they open in read-only mode. Before you or anyone else can edit such documents, they must be extracted from the folder as described in the following section.

Extracting files from a compressed folder

Because the files placed in a compressed folder automatically open in read-only mode, you may need to extract them (that is, decompress them) so that you can again edit their contents. To extract files from a compressed folder, follow these steps:

1. Open the window in Windows Explorer that contains the compressed folder whose files you want to extract.

2. Right-click the compressed folder (remember, its icon should sport a zipper down the front) and then click Extract All on its shortcut menu.

   If the Classic menus are displayed in the Explorer window, you can perform this step by clicking the compressed folder's icon and then choosing File⇨Extract All. If not, press Alt+FT.

   Windows 7 then opens an Extract Compressed (Zipped) Folders dialog box, where you designate the folder into which the extracted files are to be copied.

3. (Optional) Replace the path and the filename of the compressed folder in the Files Will Be Extracted to This Folder text box with the pathname of the folder in which you want to store the extracted (decompressed) files.

   To browse to the folder in which you want the extracted files copied, click the Browse button, select the (destination) folder in the outline of your computer system, and click OK. To extract the files in their original compressed folder, don't replace the path and filename for the compressed folder that appears in this text box. Just be aware that the only way to recompress the files that you extract in the compressed folder is to first move them out of the folder and then move them back in!

4. Click the Extract button at the bottom of the Select a Destination and Extract Files dialog box to begin extracting the files.

   As soon as Windows 7 finishes extracting the files, it opens the destination folder displaying the uncompressed files.

Selecting files and folders

To select files and folders so you can do stuff to them — stuff like copy, move, open, or print — select the file or folder icons (the small pictures identifying the folder or file). Most of the time, you click the file and folder icons in the windows to select them. Windows 7 lets you know when an icon is selected by highlighting it in a different color (normally, a light blue unless you change the Windows appearance settings).

If you change the click options in the Folder Options dialog box so that single-clicking opens an item (*see* "Changing how you select and open items" earlier in this part for details), remember that instead of clicking a folder or file icon to select it (which succeeds only in opening the item), you just hover the mouse pointer over it.

When you need to select more than one file or folder in a window, you have a choice of things to do:

- ✔ To select all the items in an Explorer window (including all drive, file, and folder icons located within it), press Ctrl+A or click the Organize button on the window's toolbar and then choose Select All from its drop-down menu.

  If the Classic menus are displayed in the Explorer window, you can also choose Edit⇨Select All on the window menu bar. If not, press Alt+EA.

- ✔ To select multiple folder or file icons that are located all over the place in the window, hold down the Ctrl key as you click each folder or file icon. (The Ctrl key adds individual icons to the selection.) If you use single-clicking to open items, you need to hover over each item as you hold down the Ctrl key (no easy feat).

- ✔ To select a series of folder or file icons that are all next to each other in the window, click the first one in the series and then hold the Shift key as you click the last icon in the series. (The Shift key adds all the icons in between the first and last one you click to the selection.) If you use single-clicking to open items, you need to hover over the first item until it's selected and then hold the Shift key as you hover over the last icon in the series. (If you think pressing Ctrl and hovering is hard, wait till you try pressing Shift and hovering.)

- ✔ If the Classic menus are displayed, you can reverse the icon selection in a window so that all the icons that aren't currently selected become selected, and all those that are currently selected become deselected by choosing Edit⇨Invert Selection. If not, you can press Alt+EI.

Note that the Invert Selection menu command is really useful when you want to select all but a few folders or files in a window: First, use one of the aforementioned methods to select the icons of the files you do *not* want selected; then choose Edit⇨Invert Selection (Alt+EI). *Voilà!* All the files in the window are selected except for those few you selected in the first place.

Copying (and moving) files and folders

Windows 7 provides two basic methods for copying files and folders from one disk to another or from one folder to another on the same disk:

✔ **Drag and drop:** You select items in one open Explorer window and then drag them to another open Explorer window (on the same or different disk), where you drop them into place.

✔ **Cut and paste:** You copy or cut selected items to the Windows Clipboard and then paste them into another folder (on the same or different disk).

Using the drag-and-drop method

The technique of moving files and folders with the drag-and-drop method is really straightforward:

1. Open two separate Explorer windows and arrange them on the Windows 7 desktop with as little overlap as possible: the first is the source Explorer window that contains the item(s) you want to move, and the second is the destination Explorer window where these items are to be moved.

To eliminate all overlap between the source and destination Explorer window and thereby make it easy to drag from one to the other, right-click the taskbar and then choose either the Show Windows Side by Side option or the Show Windows Stacked option from the shortcut menu that appears.

2. Select the item(s) you want to move in the first source Explorer window.

See "Selecting files and folders" earlier in this part for the techniques Windows 7 provides for selecting folders and files.

3. While continuing to hold down the mouse button, drag the folder/document icon representing the selected items (and showing the number of items selected) to the destination Explorer window.

4. Windows 7 displays a ScreenTip that says Move to *such and such folder* (where *such and such a folder* is the actual name of the destination folder). When you've positioned the icon somewhere within the destination Explorer window, release the mouse button to drop the items there (see Figure 2-6). They then appear in the destination window in the order (usually alphabetical by filename) that that Explorer window currently uses.

To copy files with the drag-and-drop method rather than move them, you only have to vary these foregoing steps by remembering to hold down the Ctrl key as you drag the selected items from the source Explorer window to the destination window. Windows 7 lets you know that you're copying rather than moving the selected items by displaying a + (plus) sign under the folder/document icon and displaying a Copy to *such and such folder* ScreenTip when you reach a place in the destination folder where the items being copied can be dropped.

Figure 2-6

When moving or copying files using the drag-and-drop method, you don't even have to bother opening the destination folder in its own window: Just drag the folder/document icon representing the selected items from the source Explorer window to the destination folder's icon and then drop it on this icon. Note that this drop-directly-on-the-destination-icon method works on shortcuts of other drives (both local and on your network) as well as shortcuts for folders and printers (to print the selected documents) on the Windows 7 desktop. (*See* "Creating desktop shortcuts" in Part 1.)

Keep in mind that when you drag files or folders from one drive to another, Windows 7 automatically copies the files and folders, instead of moving them. This copying means that you don't have to hold down the Ctrl key when you intend to copy them from one disk to another. It also means that you must still delete them from their original disk after making the copies if you need to free up the disk space.

Dragging and dropping items from folder to folder is great because it's really fast. This method does have a major drawback, however: It's pretty easy to drop your file icons into the wrong folder. If you forget to undo your last action (Ctrl+Z), instead of panicking when you open what you thought was the destination folder and find that your files aren't there, locate them by using the Search feature; *see* "Searching for files" later in this part.

Using the cut-and-paste method

Instead of turning to the drag-and-drop trick, you can use the cut-and-paste method, the oldest way of moving and copying items in Windows. The cut-and-paste method, as the name implies, involves two distinct processes. In the first, you cut or copy the selected files or folders to a special area of the computer memory known as the Windows Clipboard. In the second, you paste the item(s) saved on the Clipboard into the new folder.

You can perform the cut, copy, and paste commands by selecting the Cut, Copy, and Paste commands on the Organize button on the Explorer window's toolbar, or by using standard Ctrl+X (cut), Ctrl+C (copy), and Ctrl+V (paste) keyboard shortcuts.

To move or copy files by cutting and pasting (using either method), follow these steps:

1. Open the folder with Windows Explorer (Documents, Computer, or Network) that holds the subfolders or files that you're moving or copying.

2. Select all the items to be copied and then either press Ctrl+C (or choose Copy from the Organize button's drop-down menu) or press Ctrl+X (or choose Cut from the Organize button's drop-down menu).

3. Use the Navigation pane in the Explorer window to open the destination folder (that is, the one into which you're moving or copying the selected folder or file items).

   Don't forget to click the Folders button in the Navigation pane to display the hierarchy of components and folders on your computer.

4. Press Ctrl+V (or choose Paste from the Organize button's drop-down menu) to paste the items into the destination folder.

When using the cut-and-paste method to move or copy files or folders, keep in mind that you don't have to keep the folder with the files or folders you're moving or copying open during the paste part of the procedure. You can close this folder, open the folder to which you're moving or copying them, and then do the paste command. Just be sure that you don't use the Copy or Cut commands again in Windows 7 until after you've pasted these files and folders in their new location.

If the Classic menus are displayed in the Explorer window, you can also access the Cut, Copy, and Paste commands by choosing Edit➪Cut, Edit➪Copy, and Edit➪Paste respectively from the source and destination Explorer window's drop-down menus. If not, you can press Ctrl+X to cut, Ctrl+C to copy, and Ctrl+V to paste.

In addition, when the Classic menus are displayed, you have access to the special Edit➪Copy to Folder and Edit➪Move to Folder commands (or if they're not displayed, you can press Alt+EF for Copy to Folder and Alt+EV for Move to Folder). When you choose either of these menu commands (after selecting the items to be moved or copied), Windows 7 displays a Copy Items or a Move Items dialog box (depending upon which you command you choose). You then select the icon of the destination folder in the outline map of your system before clicking the Move or Copy button to perform the move or copy operation.

Keep in mind that if all you want to do is back up some files from your hard drive to a CD or DVD in your computer's CD-ROM/DVD drive (D:, E: or some other letter), you can do so with the Send To shortcut menu command. After selecting the files to copy, just right-click to open the shortcut menu attached to one of the file icons and then choose the correct drive on the Send To menu, such as DVD-RW Drive (D:). Oh, and one more thing: Don't forget to insert a blank CD-ROM or DVD or one to which you can append new files before you start this little operation.

Deleting files and folders

You need to know how to get rid of unneeded files and folders to free space on your hard drive. To delete files, folders, or shortcuts, follow these steps:

1. Open the window in Windows Explorer that holds the files or folders that need to be given the old heave-ho.

2. Select all the files, folders, or shortcuts to be deleted.

3. Press the Delete key or choose Delete from the Organize button's drop-down menu on the window's toolbar.

If the Classic menus are displayed in the Explorer window, you can also choose File➪Delete; if not, press Alt+FD. If you're really motivated, you can drag the selected items and drop them on the Recycle Bin desktop icon.

4. Click the Yes button in the Confirm File Delete or Confirm Multiple File Delete dialog box that asks whether you want to send the selected items to the Recycle Bin.

Windows 7 puts all items that you delete in the Recycle Bin, its version of the trash can. Anything you delete anywhere in Windows goes into the Recycle Bin and stays there until you either retrieve the deleted item or empty the Recycle Bin.

Note that the Recycle Bin icon is the one permanent item on the Windows desktop. To open the Recycle Bin window (see Figure 2-7), simply double-click the icon on the desktop.

Use the following tips to work efficiently with the Recycle Bin:

✓ **To fill the Recycle Bin:** Select the folders or files you no longer need, drag their icons to the Recycle Bin icon on the desktop, and drop them in.

✓ **To rescue stuff from the Recycle Bin:** Open the Recycle Bin and then select the icons for the items you want to restore. Next, click the Restore This Item button (if only one item is selected) or the Restore the Selected Items button (if multiple items are selected) on the Recycle Bin window's toolbar.

If the Classic menus are displayed, you can also choose File⇨Restore to remove the selected item or items; if not, you can press Alt+FE. Also, you can always drag the icons for the files and folders you want to save out of the Recycle Bin and drop them in the desired location.

Figure 2-7

✔ **To rescue all the stuff in the Recycle Bin:** Open the Recycle Bin and click the Restore All Items button on the Recycle Bin window's toolbar. Note that this button is replaced by the Restore This Item or Restore the Selected Items button when you select one or more items.

✔ **To empty the Recycle Bin:** Open the Recycle Bin and click the Empty the Recycle Bin button on Recycle Bin window's toolbar.

If the Classic menus are displayed, you can also choose File⇨Empty Recycle Bin. If the menus are not displayed, press Alt+FB.

Keep in mind that choosing the Empty Recycle Bin command immediately gets rid of everything in the Recycle Bin window. Don't ever empty the Recycle Bin until *after* you examine the contents and are absolutely sure that you'll never need to use any of those items ever again (or you've backed up the files on disks or some other media, such as CD-ROM or DVD discs).

If you hold down the Shift key when pressing the Delete key, Windows displays a Delete File dialog box that asks you to confirm the permanent deletion of the selected items. If you click the Yes button or press Enter, whatever you targeted for deletion does not go to the Recycle Bin, does not pass Go and does not collect $200. Rather, the item is instantly (and permanently) removed from your computer. (Take this step *only* when you want to kiss these babies goodbye forever!)

Renaming files and folders

You can rename file and folder icons directly in Windows 7 by typing over or editing the existing file or folder name, as I outline in these steps:

1. Open the folder that contains the file you want to rename in an Explorer window such as Documents or Computer.

2. Right-click the file or folder icon, and choose Rename from the shortcut menu that appears.

3. Type the new name that you want to give the folder (up to 255 characters) or edit the existing name. You can use the Delete key to remove characters and the → or ← key to move the cursor without deleting characters.

4. When you finish editing the file or folder name, press the Enter key to complete the renaming procedure.

When the file or folder name is selected for editing, typing anything entirely replaces the current name. If you want to edit the file or folder name rather than replace it, you need to click the insertion point at the place in the name that needs editing before you begin typing.

Searching for files

The Search feature provides you with an extremely efficient way to locate any program, folder, or file on your computer system. A Search text box appears in the upper-right corner of all the major Explorer windows — Computer, Documents, Network, Control Panel, Pictures, Music, and the like. (You can find a similar Search text box at the bottom of the Windows 7 Start menu, where it's labeled *Search Programs and Files.*)

Search immediately starts searching your computer system for matches to any characters you enter into one of its Search text boxes the moment you type them and displaying the results in a Search Results window (similar to the one in Figure 2-8). The feature automatically searches for matches not only in the names of programs, drives, folders, files, and so forth on your computer, but also in the *metadata* in files (that is, keywords you assign and statistics such as author, date modified, and so on that Windows and other programs automatically assign), and even in text contained in document files.

Keep in mind that, generally speaking, Search automatically searches *all* the files on your computer system for the characters you type into a search text box. If you want to search only a particular drive or folder on your computer system, you need to perform an advanced search by using the Search pane. (*See* "Doing advanced searches with search filters" later in this part.)

Figure 2-8

Adding tags for searches

Because Search automatically searches the metadata added to your files, you can make these searches much more effective by adding your own tags, including keywords and other types of search data, whenever possible.

When creating documents with application programs such as Microsoft Word or Excel 2007, you can add all kinds of your own metadata tags — including Author, Title, Subject, Category, Keywords, Status, and Comments — by opening the document and then opening its Document Properties area (Office Button➪ Prepare➪Properties). In a program such as Adobe Reader 9, you can add keywords by opening the PDF file and then selecting the Description tab of the Document Properties dialog box (File➪Properties).

For media files on your computer (music, video, and photos and other graphic images), Windows 7 actually enables you to add tags in the Preview pane that appears along the bottom of Music, Videos, and Pictures Explorer windows (after you click the Show Preview Pane button, of course). To add tags to one of these media files, all you have to do is select the file in its Explorer window, click the Edit button and then add the desired tags to the appropriate fields on the Details tab in the file's Properties dialog box.

Music, video, and graphic media files have particular metadata tags options on the Details tab of their Properties dialog boxes, such as titles, dates and time taken, and a rating between one and five stars (by clicking the appropriate star).

Doing advanced searches with search filters

Most of the time, you need to perform only simple searches in order to find the item you're looking for. Windows 7 does, however, provide Add a Search Filter options that appear in a drop-down menu box immediately beneath the Search text box when you click it. The actual search filters available vary according to the type of drive, folder, or file that's currently selected in the Explorer window.

These advanced search filters can modify searches so that they take into account certain criteria, including the following:

✔ **Date Modified:** Use this filter to search for files in a document folder by the date they were last modified.

✔ **Date Taken:** This filter searches for photos in a pictures folder by the date they were snapped.

✔ **Date Created:** Use this filter to search for files — a video file, for example — according to when the file was created. After selecting this filter, you can select a specific date from the mini-calendar that appears or a range of dates by dragging through the dates on the calendar. You can also specify a less precise search filter by selecting one of the verbal filter options that appears beneath the mini-calendar: A Long Time Ago, Earlier This Year, Earlier This Month, Last Week, Earlier This Week, or Yesterday.

✔ **Size:** With this filter, you can search for documents by the file size. Specify the file size by typing in the number of its kilobytes or megabytes in the search text box (followed by KB or MB). You can also specify a size search filter by selecting any of the size range options that appear from the drop-down list beneath the Search text box after you click the Size option: Empty (0 KB), Tiny (0–10 KB), Small (10–100 KB), Medium (100 KB–1 MB), Large (1–16 MB), Huge (16–128 MB), or Gigantic (>128 MB).

✔ **Kind:** This filter searches for documents by kind. You specify the kind of file by selecting its option from the drop-down list that appears when you click the Kind option: Calendar, Communication, Contact, Document, E-mail, Feed, Folder, Game, or Instant Message, Journal, Link, Music, Note, Picture, Program, Recorded TV, Saved Search, Task, Video, or Web History.

✔ **Type:** Not to be confused with the Kind filter, Type filter searches rely on the fact that certain file types always come with the same file extension, whether it be .pdf, .jpg, .xls, .xlsx, .doc, or .docx. You can then specify the file type by selecting the appropriate filename extension from the drop-down list that appears after you click the Type option.

✔ **Name:** As the name implies, the Name filter searches for a document by its filename by entering all or part of the filename in this text box — you can use the asterisk (*) to stand for one or more wild-card characters in the filename and a question mark (?) to stand for individual wild-card characters in the search text box after the Name filter in the Search text box.

- ✔ **Length:** Use this filter to search for a music or video file by its relative length. After selecting the Length filter, you can enter the exact length or select one of the Length options that appear in the drop-down list: Very Short (Under 1 Min), Short (1–5 Mins), Medium (5–30 Mins), Long (30–60 Mins), or Very Long (Over 60 Mins).

- ✔ **Tags:** This filter lets you search for a document by the tags assigned to it. Simply enter one or more tags after the Tags filter in the Search text box.

- ✔ **Authors:** Use this filter to search for text documents by a particular author. All you need to do is enter an author name after the Authors filter in the Search text box or select the name from the drop-down list that appears when you choose this filter. (Note that this filter is called Artists when searching audio files in any of your Music library folders. There, you use the Artists filter to find files for particular performers by entering their names after this filter.)

When creating searches with more than one filter, keep in mind that all the conditions you specify with the Date Modified, Size, Kind, Type, Name, Tags, and Authors search filters are *inclusive,* which means that all their conditions must be met in order for the types of files you've specified to be returned to your Search Results window.

Saving search results in a search folder

Instead of going through the whole rigmarole of reentering the same search criteria each time you want to find the same types of items on your computer, you can save the results of your search as a search folder. That way, you have access to the items simply by opening the search folder after selecting the Searches link in a Windows Explorer window.

To save your search results as search folder, follow these steps:

1. Click the Save Search button on Windows Explorer or Search window's toolbar.

   Windows 7 opens a Save As dialog box where you specify the name and description for your new search folder.

2. (Optional) Add other author names to the folder by clicking Authors and entering them, or add tags that identify the search folder and can be used in searching for it by clicking the Add a Tag text in the Tags field.

3. Click the Save button to create your search folder and save it in the Favorites area (that appears at the top of the Navigation pane in each Explorer window) before closing the Save As dialog box.

After saving your search results as a search folder, Windows 7 automatically re-creates the search criteria, performs the same Search, and then displays the updated results for that search each time you select the search folder in the Favorites area at the top of the Navigation pane in Windows Explorer.

Program Management

All programs that you purchase out of the box have their own setup programs that lead you through the entire installation procedure. Most of these setup programs launch automatically as soon as you place their program CD-ROMs or DVDs in your computer's CD-ROM/DVD drive.

On the rare occasion that a setup program doesn't start running on its own, you can jump-start the procedure by opening the Run window from the Start menu (just type **ru** in the Start Search text box if Run doesn't appear on the Start menu and then click its hyperlink) and then typing **setup.exe** in its Open text box before you click OK or press Enter.

After you've installed your programs on your Windows 7 computer, you can use its Installed Programs window to monitor these programs as well as to repair or remove them.

Removing or repairing a program

To remove a program installed on your computer, you need to open the Installed Programs Control Panel window. Choose Start➪Control Panel and then click the Uninstall a Program link under Programs in the Control Panel. Next, select the application name in the list displayed and then click the Uninstall button (sometimes called Uninstall/Change) on the Installed Programs window's toolbar. Next, Windows 7 may open a User Account Control dialog box, in which case you need to click the Continue button. Then click the Yes button on the alert dialog box that appears to ask whether you're sure that you want to remove the program and all its components from your computer.

If you're having trouble running one or more of the Microsoft Office programs (programs in the Microsoft Office 2003 suite or some earlier version, for example), you can try fixing the programs by clicking the Microsoft Office listing and then clicking the Change button and then selecting the Repair option followed by Continue in the Change Your Installation of Microsoft Office dialog box.

Changing the program defaults

By default, Windows 7 automatically configures particular programs to do certain tasks, such as browse the Internet, receive and send e-mail, and play audio and video files on your computer. You can, if you desire, change these program associations on your computer by opening the Set Program Access and Computer Defaults dialog box.

You open the Set Program Access and Computers Defaults dialog box by clicking Start⇨Default Programs. Next, click the Set Programs Access and Computer Defaults link in the Default Programs Control Panel window followed by the Continue button in the Permission dialog box.

The Set Program Access and Computer Defaults dialog box contains three Configuration options:

- ✔ **Microsoft Windows:** This option selects all Microsoft programs for your Internet and media playing needs.

- ✔ **Non-Microsoft:** Use this option to select all the non-Microsoft programs that you've installed on your computer for your Internet and media playing needs.

- ✔ **Custom:** The default option, Custom uses whatever Internet or media-playing program you're currently using on the computer but still offers you access to Microsoft's Internet and media software (just in case you one day see the light and decide that you want to junk your non-Microsoft browser, e-mail client, or media player in favor of Internet Explorer, Windows Mail, Windows Media Center, and Windows Media Player).

To completely change a new configuration, simply select its option in the Set Program Access and Computer Defaults dialog box and then click OK. To change only certain program associations within a configuration (especially the Custom configuration), click its expand button (the one with two >> pointing downward) and then modify individual settings within that configuration before you click OK.

Figure 2-9 shows you the Set Program Access and Computer Defaults dialog box on my computer after expanding its Custom section to display the default Web browser and default e-mail program settings.

Figure 2-9

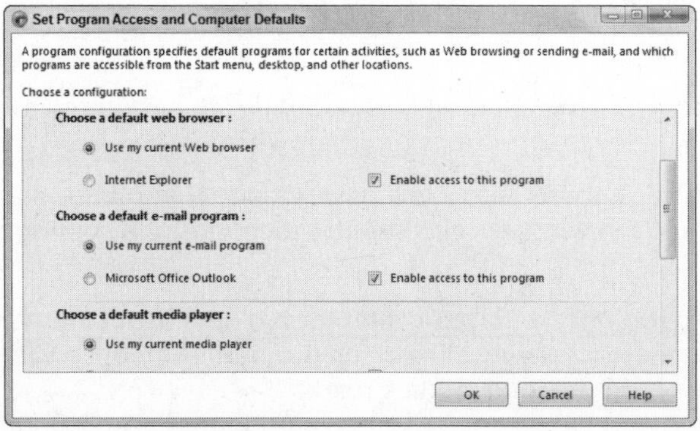

Restart, Sleep/Hibernate, Lock, Log Off, and Shut Down

After you press the computer's power button to power up the machine and start the Windows 7 operating system, the Windows Start menu contains all the other controls you need in order to switch between users, reboot the system, and, at the end of the day, power down and shut off the machine.

To the immediate right of the Search Programs and Files text box at the bottom of the Start menu, you find the Windows Power button (labeled Shut Down by default). Clicking the Windows' Power button on the Start menu is the equivalent of pressing the physical power button on your computer. Windows 7 closes all applications and open windows, while at the same time prompting you to save all unsaved changes, before shutting off your computer.

You can change the function of the Windows 7 Power button from its default of Shut Down to some other function. Right-click the Windows taskbar and then choose Properties from the shortcut menu that appears to open the Taskbar and Menu Properties dialog box. Click the Start Menu tab in this dialog box and then select the desired option from the Power Button Action drop-down list: Switch User, Log Off, Lock, Restart, Sleep, or Hibernate. Note that after selecting a new function for the Power button, Windows displays the new function's name on the button and adds the Shut Down option to the pop-up menu that appears when you click the triangular button to the immediate right of the Power button.

When you click the pop-up button to the immediate right of the Power button, Windows displays a menu with the following items:

- ✔ **Switch User:** Switches to another user account on the computer without closing your open programs and Windows processes.

- ✔ **Log Off:** Switches to another user account on the computer after closing all of your open programs and Windows processes.

- ✔ **Lock:** Locks up the computer while you're away from it (same as clicking the Lock button).

- ✔ **Restart:** Reboots the computer. (This option is often required as part of installing new software programs or Windows updates.)

- ✔ **Sleep:** Puts the computer into a low-power mode that retains all running programs and open windows in computer memory for a super-quick restart.

- ✔ **Hibernate (found only on laptop computers):** Puts the computer into a low-power mode after saving all running programs and open windows on the machine's hard drive for a quick restart.

TIP Windows 7 shows its old DOS roots by still honoring the good old three-finger salute — Ctrl+Alt+Del. When you press these keys in unison, the screen blacks out for a moment before presenting you with a blue-green screen containing the following text options: Lock This Computer, Switch User, Log Off, Change a Password, and Start Task Manager.

In addition to these text options, this screen contains the following buttons:

- **Cancel:** Returns you to the Windows 7 desktop along with all of your open program windows.

- **Ease of Access (the blue button in the lower-left corner of the screen):** Opens the Ease of Access dialog box where you can select among various accessibility settings for making the computer easier to use for those with visual and other physical impairments.

- **Power (the red button):** Shuts down the computer. This button is equipped with its own pop-up button in the lower-right corner of the screen. Note that the items on the menu attached to this pop-up button include Restart, Sleep, Hibernate (on a laptop), and Shut Down.

Windows Explorer

Windows Explorer (not to be confused with Internet Explorer, its Internet equivalent) provides you the means for navigating your computer system by giving you access to all aspects of your computer system from your user files (simply called documents) to the Control Panel.

You can access one of the Windows Explorer windows by clicking any of the following links that appear in the right column of the Start menu:

- **Documents:** Opens the Documents library, which typically contains the text and data type files (also known as document files) you create — this is the default location for saving document files for programs such as Microsoft Word and Excel and is the Windows 7 equivalent of My Documents in Windows XP.

- **Pictures:** Opens the Pictures library, which typically contains the digital photographs and other types of graphic files you store on your computer — this is the Windows 7 equivalent of My Pictures in Windows XP.

- **Music:** Opens the Music library, which typically contains the music audio files (in all different audio formats, including MP3, WMA, and WAV) you store on your computer — this is the Windows 7 equivalent of My Music in Windows XP.

✔ **Games:** Opens the Games window, which contains all the games that come installed with Windows Vista. (*See* "Games" in Part 6.)

✔ **Computer:** Opens the Computer window, which displays all the local and mapped network drives on your computer as well as all peripheral devices currently connected to it. (*See* "Disk Management" earlier in this part.)

✔ **Control Panel:** Opens the Control Panel, which displays all the settings you can change on your computer system. (*See* "Control Panel" in Part 5.)

✔ **Devices and Printers:** Opens the Devices and Printers window, which shows all the various devices (such as cameras and mice) currently connected to your computer along with all the installed printers.

 By default, the Windows 7 Start menu doesn't contain an option for opening an Explorer window for your network. If you want to add such an option, you can do so. Right-click the Windows taskbar and then choose Properties from the shortcut menu that appears to open the Taskbar and Menu Properties dialog box. Click the Start Menu tab in this dialog box and then click the Customize button to open the Customize Start Menu dialog box. Once you're there, select the Homegroup check box (if you've set up a peer-to-peer home network) or the Network check box (if your computer is part of a local area network) before clicking OK. (*See* "Connect to a Network" in Part 3 for information on adding your computer to a network.)

Changing the display of an Explorer window

You can control how the information returned to any Explorer window is displayed through the use of the Layout item found on the Organize button's drop-down menu in combination with the pop-up slider attached to the Change Your View pop-up button on the window's toolbar. (This pop-up button is the third one in on the right side of the toolbar, and its icon changes to match the type of folder and file view currently selected in the window.)

The Layout item on the Organize button's drop-down menu contains the following submenu:

✔ **Menu Bar:** Turns on and off the display of the menus File through Help.

✔ **Details Pane:** Turns on and off the display of the Details pane along the bottom of the window. The Details pane gives you information about the currently selected item in the window and often enables you to add searchable information through the use of its Edit link.

✔ **Preview Pane:** Turns on and off the display of the Preview pane on the right side of the window. The Preview pane displays a live view of whatever folder or file is currently selected in the window.

✔ **Navigation Pane:** Turns on and off the display of the Navigation pane on the left side of the window. You can use the Navigation pane to open new folders on your computer system

✔ **Library Pane:** Turns on and off the display of the Library pane immediately above the file display of the files in one of your libraries (Documents, Music, Pictures, and Videos). The Library pane shows you information about the library's contents and also enables you to change the order in which its files are displayed.

The pop-up slider attached to the Change Your View drop-down button contains the following view options (you can also toggle through the Large Icons, List, Details, and Tile options in succession by repeatedly clicking the Views button):

✔ **Extra Large Icons:** Displays the folders and files in the window as really huge icons with their names displayed as captions beneath the icons.

✔ **Large Icons:** Displays the folders and files in the window as fairly large icons with their names displayed beneath the icons.

✔ **Medium Icons:** Displays the folders and files in the window as medium-sized icons with their names displayed beneath the icons.

✔ **Small Icons:** Displays the folders and files in the window as fairly small icons with their names displayed as captions to the right side of the icons.

✔ **List:** Displays icons followed by the folder names and filenames in a single-column list.

✔ **Details:** Displays information about the folders and files in the window in a strict columnar format that includes Name, Date Modified, Type, Authors, and Tags. Note that you can widen and narrow these columns as needed by dragging the borders of their labels to the left and right.

✔ **Tiles:** Displays the folders and files in the window as icons with text giving their names and file sizes arranged in one or two vertical columns.

✔ **Content:** Displays the information about the folders and files in a two-column format, the first of which contains an icon or thumbnail identifying the type of file and the second of which displays file information: the date modified and file size in the case of text files, date taken and file size in the case of photos, and the length and file size in the case of music and video files.

Keep in mind that when selecting any one of the Icons options, you can use the Change Your View drop-down button's slider to select sizes in between the preset sizes utilized by selecting the Extra Large Icons, Large Icons, Medium Icons, or Small Icons option.

Sorting and filtering items in an Explorer window

When you select the Details option on the Change Your View pop-up button's slider in an Explorer window, Windows displays column headings such Name, Date Modified, Type, and Size buttons at the top of the display area.

You can use any of these buttons to sort or filter the current contents of any Explorer window. To sort the contents, simply click the button that you want to use in sorting: once to sort the list of folders and files in descending order (Z to A for text and most recent to least recent for dates) indicated by a triangle pointing downward in the middle above the name of the column, and a second time to return the files to their original ascending order (A to Z for text and least recent to most recent for dates) indicated by a triangle pointing upward.

To filter the contents of an Explorer window to just those types of folders and files you want to see, use any of the different buttons (Name through Size) to open the accompanying drop-down menu and then select the check boxes for all the types of folders and files you want displayed.

For example, Figure 2-10 shows you my Documents window after I filtered its contents by limiting the display to those files created between January 2006 and December 2007. I did the filtering by clicking the Select a Date or Date Range check box and then clicking the date in the title bar of the mini-calendar right underneath (to change from days in a month to months in a year) and, finally, dragging through these months in the mini-calendar. As soon as I did that, Windows 7 filtered out all folders and files except for those that I worked with sometime during the period of these two years.

Figure 2-10

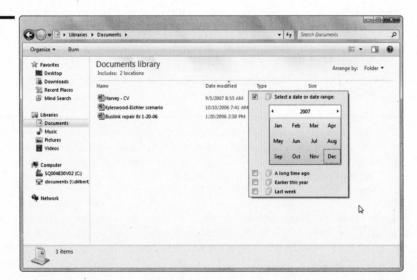

Note that when filtering the contents of a window, you can select settings from more than one button's drop-down menu to refine the results. For example, if I want to see only the Excel workbook files I modified during this two-year period, I would select not only these dates on the Date Modified column's drop-down menu, but also the Microsoft Office Excel 97-2003 Worksheet check box on the Type column's drop-down menu.

To restore an Explorer window to its previous contents after filtering it, simply remove the check marks from all the check boxes on the different buttons' drop-down menus that you selected.

Networking

Windows 7 is right at home with all types of private networking currently in use, everything from the kind of server-less, peer-to-peer networks you set in the home (referred to as a homegroup) to small-scale local area networks (LANs) and wide area networks (WANs) in business. Networks like the one shown in this figure enable your various computers to share resources such as network printers, scanners, and, most importantly, broadband connections to the Internet.

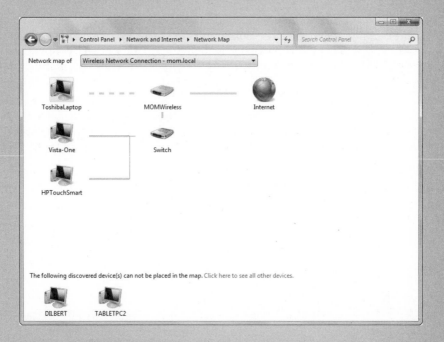

In this part . . .

- ✔ Connecting to a Dialup, VPN, or Wireless Network
- ✔ Viewing and Exploring the Computers on the Network
- ✔ Managing Network Connections for Wired and Wireless Networks
- ✔ Viewing a Map of the Network
- ✔ Managing and Setting Up Your Network Connections

Connect to a Network

Types of connections to private networks include the more traditional Ethernet connection, with its network adapters and cabling, as well as the newer, increasingly popular wireless connection (commonly referred to as Wi-Fi), with its wireless network adapters and access points (also known as *hotspots*).

Having so many options may seem like a recipe for networking disaster, but fortunately Windows 7 is super at detecting existing private networks during installation and often requires little or no additional network setup. The topics covered in this part of the book discuss the networking features in Windows 7, how you use them to create networking connections, and how you maintain them.

If the computer running the Windows 7 operating system connects to your network via a dialup, VPN (virtual private network), or wireless connection, you can use the Connect to a Network option in the Network and Sharing Center (Start⇨Control Panel⇨View Network Status) either to disconnect from a current connection or to make a new connection.

When you click the Connect to a Network link in the Network and Sharing Center, Windows 7 opens a dialog box similar to the one shown in Figure 3-1. By default, Windows shows all the networks to which your computer is or can be connected.

Figure 3-1

Currently connected to:	
mom.local Internet access	
Wireless Network Connection	∧
MOMWireless	**Connected**
PBL794	
2WIRE989	
Apple Network DAC	
belkin54g	
Open Network and Sharing Center	

To connect to a listed network, click its name and then click the Connect button. (Note that the button only appears *after* you click the name of the network.) If the network requires you to supply a key, Windows prompts you to enter your network security key in the Connect to a Network dialog box that then appears, assuming that your wireless connection requires some type of authentication — select the Hide Characters check box if you don't want the characters you type displayed in the Security Key text box. After you successfully enter your security key and click OK, click the Connect button to have Windows 7 use the key in establishing the connection.

To disconnect from a network, click the network name in this dialog box and then click the Disconnect button (that then appears). Windows 7 then prompts you to confirm your disconnection in the Connect to a Network dialog box by clicking the Disconnect link, after which you can click the Close button.

If you tend to work with network settings quite a bit, you may want to permanently add the various network options to your Windows 7 Start menu so that you don't have to search for their links. These options include Connect To (to view or change network connections), Network (to open the Network window to see all the devices on your local area network), and Homegroup (to see all the devices on your homegroup). To add such networking options, right-click the Windows taskbar to open the Taskbar and Start Menu Properties dialog box. Then click the Customize button on the Start tab. Continue by selecting the check boxes for the network options you want to add to the Start menu (Connect To, Network, or Homegroup) and then click OK twice, first to close the Customize Start Menu dialog box and a second time to close the Taskbar and Start Menu Properties dialog box.

Change Adapter Settings

You can use the Network Connections window to manage any of the Ethernet and wireless connections you use to connect your computer to the company's network or the Internet. To open this window, click the Change Adapter Settings link that appears in the Navigation pane of your computer's Network and Sharing Center window (opened by choosing Start⇨Control Panel⇨View Network Status and Tasks).

When you click the Change Adapter Settings link, Windows 7 opens a Network Connections window similar to the one shown in Figure 3-2. This window shows all the wired and wireless networks that your computer attempts to automatically access whenever you turn on your computer.

To change any of the settings for a particular network connection displayed in this window, right-click the connection setting and then select the appropriate option from the shortcut menu that appears (Disable, Connect/Disconnect, Status, Diagnose, and so on). Select the Diagnose option when you're having trouble using a particular connection to get online and you want to see whether Windows can suggest ways to fix the problem. Select the Properties option when you need to view or change any of the networking or sharing settings. Note, however, that you must have administrator user status in order to open up the Properties dialog box for any of your computer's network connections.

Figure 3-2

Manage Wireless Networks

If your computer uses a Wi-Fi adapter to connect to your company's network as well as to the Internet, you can use the Manage Wireless Networks link that appears in the Navigation pane of your computer's Network and Sharing Center window (opened by choosing Start⇨Control Panel⇨View Network Status and Tasks).

When you click the Manage Wireless Networks link, Windows 7 opens a Manage Wireless Networks window similar to the one shown in Figure 3-3. This window shows all the wireless networks that your computer attempts to automatically access when the computer (assuming it's equipped with a wireless networking card) is in range of the network, along with the type of security it uses.

Modifying the order in which Windows 7 automatically connects to wireless networks

To modify the order in which your computer tries to connect to one of the available wireless networks listed in the Manage Wireless Networks window (when you have more than one network to choose from and want to promote the use of one over another in the list), all you have to do is drag its network icon to a new position in the list. (Move it up to the top of the list to promote it as the first network to try to connect to, or drag it down to the bottom to demote it as the last network to try to connect to.)

Figure 3-3

You can also change the position of a wireless connection in your listing by clicking it in the Manage Wireless Networks window and then clicking either the Move Up or Move Down buttons that appear on the toolbar when you have multiple networks listed.

Manually adding a new wireless network

Sometimes, you'll want to manually add a wireless network for which you're currently out of range to the list in the Manage Wireless Networks window so that Windows 7 can automatically connect to it when you do come in range.

To add a new wireless network to the Manage Wireless Networks window, follow these steps:

1. Open the Network and Sharing Center window by choosing Start⇨ Control Panel⇨View Network Status and Tasks.

2. Click the Manage Wireless Networks link in the Navigation pane of the Network and Sharing Center window to open the Manage Wireless Networks window. (Refer to Figure 3-3.)

3. Click the Add button on the extreme left of the Manage Wireless Networks window toolbar to open the How Do You Want to Add a Network? dialog box.

4. Click the Manually Create a Network Profile option to open the Manually Connect to a Wireless Network dialog box shown in Figure 3-4.

Figure 3-4

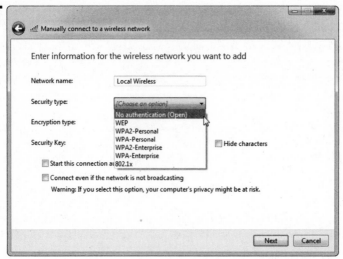

5. Enter the name of the wireless network in the Network Name text box.

6. If the wireless network is secured, select the type of security used (WEP, WPA-Personal, WPA2-Personal, WPA-Enterprise, WPA2-Enterprise, or 802.11x) in the Security Type drop-down list that currently contains No Authentication (Open).

   WEP (Wired Equivalent Privacy) and WPA (Wi-Fi Protected Access) are two security settings currently in use. Of the two, WEP is older and less reliable. WPA2 (also known as 802.11i) is the latest version of WPA security for wireless networks. The WPA-Personal settings are the ones most often used by home and small business wireless networks.

7. If you select WPA2-Personal or WPA2-Enterprise as the Security Type and your wireless network uses TKIP rather than AES-type encryption, click TKIP in the Encryption Type drop-down list.

   AES (Advanced Encryption Standard) is a block-type cipher adopted by the U.S. government. TKIP (Temporary Key Integrity Protocol) is an older security protocol created to correct deficiencies in the WEP security standard.

8. Click in the Security Key/Passphrase text box and enter the security key or passphrase assigned to the type of security and encryption used by your wireless network.

   WEP security keys are normally from 5 to 13 case-sensitive characters or 10 to 26 hexadecimal case-sensitive characters. WPA and WPA2 security keys contain 8 to 63 case-sensitive characters. To display the characters in the Security Key/Passphrase text box as you type them, select the Display Characters check box.

9. (Optional) By default, Windows 7 automatically connects to the network when the computer comes into range. If you'd prefer to control when your computer connects to the network each time the computer's in range (using the Connect To option), deselect the Start Connection Automatically check box.

10. (Optional) To have Windows 7 connect to the in-range network even when the computer doesn't detect that it's broadcasting (so that Windows will automatically use the network as soon it does start broadcasting), select the Connect Even If the Network Is Not Broadcasting check box.

11. Click the Next button.

    Windows opens a version of the Manually Connect to a Network dialog box displaying a Successfully Added message along with a Connect To and Change Connection Settings option.

12. Select the Connect To option if you now want to connect by using the new wireless connection. Click the Change Connection Settings option to open the Wireless Network Properties dialog box for the new connection (where you make modifications to the Connection or Security settings). Otherwise, click the Close button to return to the Manage Wireless Networks button.

After you close the Manually Connect to a Wireless Network dialog box, Windows 7 displays the name of the new wireless network connection at the top of the list in the Manage Wireless Networks window. You can then adjust the order in which Windows 7 uses this connection by dragging it down or demoting it by clicking the Move Down button on the toolbar.

Removing an unused network from the list

To remove a wireless network that you no longer use from the list, click its network icon in the Manage Wireless Networks window and then click the Remove button on the window's toolbar. Windows 7 then displays a Warning dialog box cautioning you that if you proceed by clicking OK, you'll no longer be able to connect to the wireless network automatically.

Network Access

The Network Explorer window (similar to the one shown in Figure 3-5) displays all the computers currently connected to the network and gives you access to their files (assuming that the network file sharing, printer sharing and discovery settings are enabled — *see* "Turning on File Sharing, Network Discovery, and Public folder sharing" that follows for details). To open this window, open any Explorer window (such as Documents or Computer from the Windows Start menu) and then click the Network icon that appears near the bottom of its Navigation pane. Windows 7 then replaces the normal display of the folders and files in the selected window with a display of the network computers and devices.

Figure 3-5

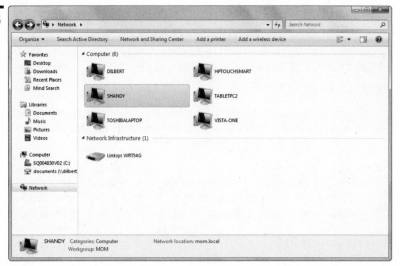

Figure 3-5 shows you the shared computers currently connected to my local area network. Note that all six computers (including TOSHIBALAPTOP, the computer on which this screenshot was taken) are part of the same domain called mom.local (of which DILBERT happens to be the name of the network server).

Icons for the computers connected to your network for which File Sharing (in computers running pre-Vista/Windows 7) or Discovery and Sharing hasn't been turned on do *not* show up in the Network window even when the computers are turned on and connected to the network.

Turning on File Sharing, Network Discovery, and Public folder sharing

You need to turn on file sharing, printer sharing and network discovery for your particular type of network (homegroup/workgroup or domain) from the Advanced Sharing Settings window (similar to the one shown in Figure 3-6) before users on the network can access their files and printers.

File and printer sharing enables network users to make use of the particular files in the folders you choose to share on your computer as well as access any printer directly connected to your computer (provided that printer is turned on and it's not offline). Network discovery enables other computers on the network to be able to see your computer as well as its printer on your network.

Figure 3-6

To open the Advanced Sharing Settings window, click Start⇨Control Panel⇨ View Network Status and Tasks⇨Change Advanced Sharing Settings. Then follow these general steps:

1. Click the expand button (the one with the greater than symbol pointing downward) for the type of network for which you want to enable file sharing (a Home or Work network or a Domain network).

2. Click the Turn on Network Discovery and File and Printer Sharing option buttons, if they're not already selected.

3. (Optional) To enable network users to share the files you place in the Public folders in your libraries (Public Documents, Public Music, Public Pictures, and so on), click the Turn On Sharing so Anyone with Network Access Can Read or Write Files in the Public Folders option button.

   See "Sharing files with Public folders" later in this part for details.

4. Click the Save Changes button to put your file and printer sharing changes as well as your network discovery changes into effect, close the Advanced Sharing Settings window and finally return to the Network and Sharing Center window.

Sharing files with the Share With menu

After you have enabled the File and Printer Sharing settings as well as the Network Discovery settings for your network, you can share particular folders and files on your computer using the options on their Share With shortcut menus. To do start sharing, follow these two steps:

1. Open an Explorer window such as Documents or Computer, then right-click the folder with the files or the particular file you want to share before you position the mouse pointer on the Share With item on its shortcut menu.

   Windows then displays a continuation menu with options specific to the type of network your computer's on (homegroup or workgroup/domain).

2. To share the folder or file with every user on your homegroup, click Homegroup (Read) to enable them to open the file(s) or Homegroup (Read/Write) to enable them to open, modify, or even delete the file(s).

   To share the folder or file with specific users on your homegroup or to share files on a workgroup/domain type network, click the Specific People item instead. Windows then opens the File Sharing wizard dialog box, where you choose the people on your network to share the file(s) with before you click the Share button (at which time, you may be prompted to enter and verify your administrator password).

   After you click the Share button after designating all the users, Windows 7 confirms that your folder or file is shared in the File Sharing window, and you can then click the Done button to close the window. Before you click Done, though, you can e-mail a link to the shared folder or item to all your designated users by clicking the E-mail link in this window (to open a new message in your e-mail program where you can select their e-mail addresses). You can also copy the link to the Windows clipboard so that you can then paste in other documents or e-mails that you send at a later time by clicking the Copy link.

Sharing files with Public folders

In addition to sharing folders and files via the Share With option, you can also share the folders and files with other network users by placing them in one of the Public folders on your computer. When you first start using Windows 7, the Public folder sharing is turned off so that no Public folders are displayed in the various libraries on your computer (*see* "File, Folder, and Library Management" in Part 2). However, after turning on Public folder sharing (as outlined in the steps in the earlier section "Turning on File Sharing, Network Discovery, and Public folder sharing" in this part), Windows automatically adds Public folders to the various default libraries that appear in the Navigation pane (Public Documents, Public Music, Public Pictures, and Public Videos).

To open these Public folders in your Documents or Computer Explorer window (as shown in Figure 3-7), click the expand button (the triangle pointing to the right) that appears next to their names in the Navigation pane, before you click the Public version of the folder. Then, to share any folders and files with network users who have access to your computer, you then simply copy or move said folders or files into these open Public folders.

Figure 3-7

Sharing drives and system files with Advanced Sharing

To be able to share the folders and files on an entire computer drive with network users or the Windows 7 system files on your computer, you need to the use Advanced Sharing option by following these steps:

1. Choose Start➪My Computer to open the My Computer window.

2. Right-click the hard drive icon for the drive whose files you want to share and then position the mouse pointer on Share With item on its shortcut menu before you click Advanced Sharing on the continuation menu that appears.

   Windows opens the Properties dialog box for the drive, with the Sharing tab selected.

3. Click the Advanced Sharing button near the bottom of the Sharing tab of the Properties dialog box.

   Windows opens the Advanced Sharing dialog box.

4. Select the Share This Folder check box in the Advanced Sharing dialog box.

5. (Optional) Click in the Shared Name text box and enter the name you want to appear. (Windows selects the disk's drive letter as the default share name.)

6. (Optional) To limit the number of users who can simultaneously access the folders and files on the drive you're sharing to a number other than 20 (the default), enter a new value in the Limit the Number of Simultaneous Users To combo box or use its spinner buttons to select it.

7. (Optional) If you want to give permission to other users who have access to the network to change the files in the folders on the disk you're sharing, click the Permission button to open the Permissions dialog box for the drive and then use the Allow and Deny check boxes to specify the level of control to each group or user that you add to the Group or User Names list box, then click OK to close this dialog box and return to the Advanced Sharing dialog box.

8. Click the OK button to close the Advanced Sharing dialog box and then click Close to close the Properties dialog box and begin sharing the drive on the network (indicated in the Computer window by the appearance of the hand underneath the drive icon).

Windows closes the Properties dialog box, and the next time you open the My Computer window, the icon for the drive you've just shared will have a Windows icon with the tiny heads of two people, indicating that it's now being shared.

When a computer on the network is running Windows 7 or Vista, rather than Windows XP or some earlier version of Windows, the Network Discovery and File Sharing settings for that computer must still be enabled in order for that computer's icon to appear in the Network window.

Opening and exploring shared computers on the network

You can open any of the computers displayed in the Network window and access their files in whatever drives and folders are shared on that computer. To do start exploring shared items, double-click the computer's icon in the Network window, or right-click it and then choose the Open (or Open in a New Window) item from the shortcut menu that appears.

Windows 7 then opens a window showing all the shared drives, folders, and devices such as shared printers (which you can then open by double-clicking their icons). Figure 3-8 shows you the window that opens when I double-click the SHANDY computer icon shown in the Network window in Figure 3-4. As you can see, this window contains a folder for the shared C: drive on this computer, its ShareDocs folder, and a couple of printers.

If you find yourself accessing the same files in a particular folder on a network computer or network server on a regular basis, consider *mapping* that folder as a local drive on your computer. That way, instead of having to open the folder via the Network window, you can access the folder quickly and directly from the

Computer window (Start⇨Computer), where it appears as though it were a local drive. The best part is that you can have Windows 7 map this folder as a local drive in the Computer window each and every time that you boot the computer so that you have to perform the actual mapping procedure only one time. *See* "Mapping a network folder as a local drive" in Part 2 for details.

Figure 3-8

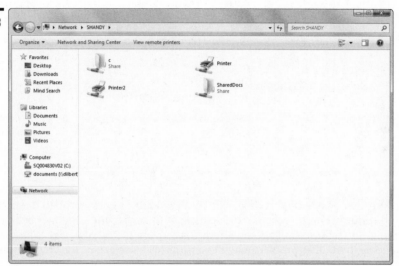

Network and Sharing Center

The Windows 7 Network and Sharing Center enables you to view at a glance the status of your networks as well as the connections they utilize. To open a Network and Sharing Center window similar to the one shown in Figure 3-9, choose Start⇨Control Panel⇨View Network Status and Tasks.

The Network and Sharing Center window contains three sections:

- ✔ **Schematic (at the top):** Shows how your computer (marked This Computer) is connected to the network and the Internet. Questionable connections are indicated in the map by exclamation points in a yellow triangle, whereas breaks in the connections are indicated by red *X*s.

- ✔ **View Your Active Networks:** Shows how your computer is connected to the network as well as the nature of that network. (*Private* indicates home or business networks that are not open to the general public; *Public* stands for networks that broadcast in public places such as cafes and airports.)

- ✔ **Change Your Networking Settings:** Displays a list of links that you can follow to change how you connect to your network.

Figure 3-9

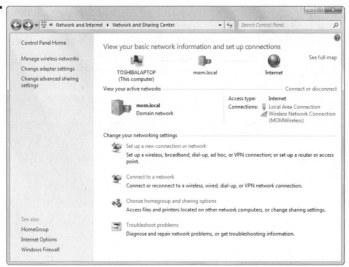

If you find some sort of trouble with your computer's connection to the network or to the Internet in the schematic displayed at the top of the window, click the yellow triangle with the exclamation point or the red *X* in the map to have Windows 7 diagnose the particular problem and, in some cases, even repair the connection.

Network Map

In addition to the simple schematic that Windows 7 displays at the top of the Network and Sharing Center window (showing your computer's basic connection to the network and Internet), you can have Windows display a more detailed network map. To display it, click the See Full Map link that appears in the upper-right corner of the Network Center window.

Figure 3-10 shows you the complete Network Map that Windows 7 created in a Network Map window when I clicked the See Full Map link in the Network and Sharing Center window shown in Figure 3-10. This detailed map traces all the intermediary steps followed by the three computers in my office: the Vista-One and HP TouchSmart computers running Windows Vista and the Toshiba Laptop running Windows 7.

According to the map in Figure 3-10, the Toshiba laptop connects to the network via a wireless connection (indicated by the dashes in the schematic) to a wireless access point connection called MOMWireless, whereas the two Vista computers connect directly to an Ethernet switch. All traffic routed by the Ethernet switch then goes directly to a broadband cable modem via that MOMWireless access point, which provides the Internet access to the network.

Figure 3-10

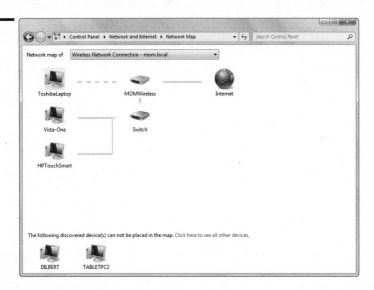

REMEMBER

Keep in mind that network computers running versions of the Windows operating system prior to Vista do not show up in the full map Windows 7 creates in the Network Map window.

TIP

Just as with the simple map shown at the top of the Network and Sharing Center window, if you find some sort of trouble is indicated in the connections shown in the full network map, simply click the yellow triangle with the exclamation point or the red *X* in the full map to have Windows 7 diagnose the particular problem and, hopefully, even repair the connection.

Set Up a New Connection or Network

Windows 7 makes it easy to set up a connection to an existing network as well as to a new peer-to-peer or ad hoc network, called a *homegroup,* so that you can share files, peripheral devices such as printers and scanners, and even the Internet.

To set up a network connection, click the Set Up a New Connection or Network link in the Network and Sharing Center window (Start⇨Control Panel⇨ View Network Status and Tasks). Windows 7 then opens the Set Up a Connection or Network dialog box, similar to the one shown in Figure 3-11 (except you may have slightly different options if your computer doesn't have wireless access), where you select the type of connection to create before clicking the Next button:

 ✔ **Connect to the Internet:** Choosing this option opens the Connect to the Internet dialog box, where you select the type of connection (wireless, broadband [PPPoE] or dialup) to use. Next, specify the information required for you to log on to the Internet service provider (ISP) or wireless network for the type of connection you select.

 ✔ **Set Up a Wireless Router or Access Point:** This option leads to a wizard that walks you through the steps of configuring a new wireless router or access point.

 ✔ **Set Up a Dial-Up Connection:** Using this option opens the Set Up a Dial-Up Connection dialog box, where you enter the dialup information for your ISP, including the dialup phone number, username, and password.

 ✔ **Connect to a Workplace:** Using this option opens the Connect to a Workplace dialog box, where you choose between using a VPN or dialup connection for connecting. If you click the Use My Internet Connection (VPN) button, a Connect to a Workplace dialog box opens, where you enter the Internet address and destination name you use to log on to the network at your workplace as provided by the network's administrator or your company's IT department. If you click the Dial Directly button, a Connect to Workplace dialog box opens, where you enter the dialup information for your workplace's ISP, including the dialup phone number, username, and password.

If you're running Windows 7 on a laptop computer equipped with wireless networking, the Set Up a Connection or Network dialog box doesn't contain the Connect to Workplace option. Instead, it contains the following two options:

 ✔ **Manually Connect to a Wireless Network:** This option enables you to select a network that isn't automatically detected (either because it's not currently broadcasting or because it's Network Discovery setting isn't turned on) or create a new wireless connection by using a different wireless network adapter installed on your computer.

 ✔ **Set Up a Wireless Ad Hoc (Computer to Computer) Network:** You can use this option to create a temporary network connection between two wireless laptop computers for sharing files, peripherals, and the Internet. (*Note:* The laptops must be within 30 feet of one another.)

Figure 3-11

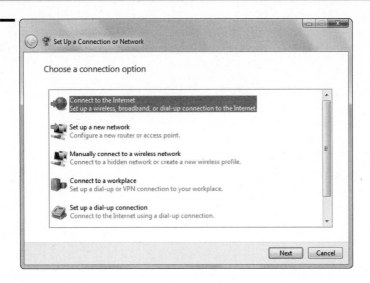

Communications

Windows 7 offers you some pretty exciting communication features in the form of a brand-new version of its award-winning Internet Explorer (version 8, shown in the following figure) and its latest version of Speech Recognition. However, if you want to add first-rate e-mail and instant messaging to Windows 7, you now need to download Windows Live Mail and Windows Live Messenger from the Web as part of the Windows Live Essentials. (*See* Part 8 for more on Windows Live Mail and Messenger.)

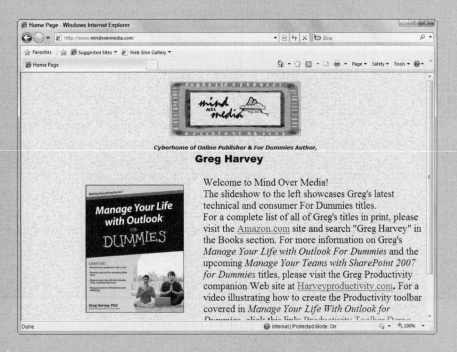

In this part . . .

- ✔ Browsing the Web with Internet Explorer 8
- ✔ Using Windows 7's Speech Recognition
- ✔ Changing the Text-to-Speech Settings
- ✔ Faxing and Scanning Documents with Windows Fax and Scan

Internet Explorer 8

Windows 7 includes Windows Internet Explorer 8 (IE 8), which enables you to browse Web pages anywhere on the Internet. This most recent version of the Microsoft Web browser is equipped with all the latest and greatest features for helping you find, visit, and retrieve any online information that might interest you.

Two basic steps are involved in browsing Web pages with the Internet Explorer 8 browser:

- Connecting to the Internet

- Going to the Web page

Windows 7 makes it a snap to launch Internet Explorer 8: All you do is click the Internet Explorer Quick Launch button (the one with *e* to the immediate right of the Start button) on the Windows 7 taskbar.

You can also launch Internet Explorer 8 from a folder window, such as Documents or Computer. When you type the Web page's address (referred to as URL, or Universal Resource Locator, as in `www.dummies.com`) in the address bar of one of these windows and then press Enter, page.

Connecting to the Internet

You connect to the Internet either with a dialup modem or a cable or DSL modem connection (all of which use a modem directly connected to your computer), or with a connection to a LAN that's connected to the Internet through some sort of high-speed telephone line, such as a T1 or T3 line.

When you connect to the Internet via a dialup connection (as you might still have to do at home), your modem must call up an Internet service provider (ISP), such as America Online (AOL), whose high-speed telephone lines and fancy switching equipment provide you with access to the Internet and all the online services (for a fee, of course).

When you connect to the Internet via a cable or DSL modem or a LAN (as is becoming more and more common from home as well as from work), you don't have to do anything special to get connected to the Internet: You have Internet access any time you turn on your computer and launch Internet Explorer.

To configure a connection to the Internet, choose Start⇨Control Panel⇨View Network Status and Tasks to open the Network and Sharing Center window. There, click the Set Up a Connection or Network link to open the Set Up a Connection or Network dialog box, where you click the link for the type of connection. *See* "Set Up a New Connection or Network" in Part 3 for more information.

Launching Internet Explorer 8

To launch Internet Explorer 8, click the Internet Explorer button on the Windows taskbar to the immediate right of the Start button. The first time you launch Internet Explorer 8, you're connected to a Windows Live page (see Figure 4-1 with the Favorites/Feeds/History Explorer bar pinned to the screen), where you can download a bunch of great utilities for instant messaging, e-mailing, blogging, and organizing your photos and videos. (The whole set of utilities is known collectively as Windows Live Essentials.)

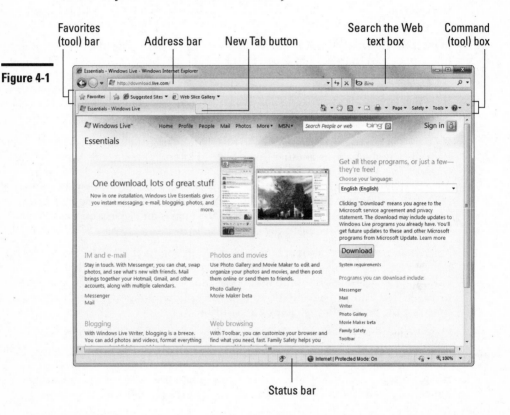

Figure 4-1

Status bar

 TIP   When newly installed, Internet Explorer 8 doesn't display the good old menu bar at the top, File through Help. To temporarily bring back the menu bar so you can perform a particular menu command, first press the Alt key. You can then complete the command sequence by typing the hot key letters assigned to the other menu items. To permanently bring back the menu bar, click the Tools button on the far right side of IE 8 toolbar and then choose Toolbars⇨Menu Bar from the drop-down menu that appears.

Adding and changing home pages

When you click the Home button in Internet Explorer 8 — the button sporting an image of a tiny house — the browser immediately opens whatever page's Web address is listed as the home page (the start page which the browser goes to each time you launch it). To change this home page, navigate to the Web page you want to use as your new home page. Click the drop-down button attached to the Home button followed and then choose Add or Change Home Page from the button's drop-down menu. Choosing this option opens the Add or Change Home Page dialog box. Then, click the Use This Webpage as Your Only Home Page option button before you click the Yes button to close this dialog box.

In Internet Explorer 8, you can have more than one Web page designated as a home page and therefore assigned to the additional home page tabs. (**See** "Using Internet Explorer 8 tabs" later in this part.) If you want to add another home page, open the Web page you want to add as a home page in Internet Explorer and click the Add This Webpage to Your Home Page Tabs option button in the Add or Change Home Page dialog box. Then click the Yes button.

Figure 4-2 illustrates how this works. In this figure, I'm just about to add the Google Web site's home page as another home page in Internet Explorer 8. After clicking the Add This Webpage to Your Home Page Tabs option button when the Google page is displayed, from then on Internet Explorer 8 automatically displays both the MSN.com and Google page (on separate tabs) whenever I launch this Web browser. That way, I can have a quick gander at the latest news and gossip on the MSN.com home page before switching to the Google tab to perform my next Web search.

After you create an additional home page, when you next click the Home button, Internet Explorer 8 then adds a tab for this additional home page that automatically appears to the right of the first home tab each time you launch this Web browser. Then all you have to do to open one of the home pages is click its tab or select the page with the Quick Tabs button.

Keep in mind that if you ever want to remove a home page and its tab from Internet Explorer 8, you can do so by first choosing Remove from the Home button's drop-down menu and then clicking the page to remove — Home Page, Home Page (2), Home Page (3), and so on — from the submenu. Finally, click Yes in the Delete Home Page dialog box to confirm its removal.

Browsing the Web

After your connection to the Internet is made and the home page appears in the browser's window, you're free to begin browsing other pages on the World Wide Web by doing any of the following:

    ✔ **Entering the Uniform Resource Locator (URL)** of the Web page in the address bar and pressing Enter or clicking the Go To button (the one with the right-pointing arrowhead that appears as soon as you begin typing the URL in the address bar).

Figure 4-2

✔ **Clicking hyperlinks** on the currently displayed Web page that take you to other Web pages, either on the same Web site or on another Web site.

✔ **Selecting a bookmarked Web page** that appears in the Favorites center Explorer bar on its Favorites tab (Ctrl+Shift+I), or a page you've recently visited on the History tab (Ctrl+Shift+H). *See* "Bookmarking Web sites as favorites" later in this part for details on how to add Web pages to the Favorites menu.

✔ **Carry out a search using the Bing Search text box** to the right of the address bar in order to display hyperlinks for the home pages of Web sites that fit your search criteria, such as "IRA investments" or, better yet, "Hawaiian vacations." *See* "Searching from the Bing Search text box" later in this part for details on searching.

Note that Internet Explorer 8 automatically displays the title of the Web page you're visiting in the current tab as well as on the Windows Internet Explorer program's title bar. *See* "Using Internet Explorer 8 tabs" later in this part for information on adding tabs for the pages you visit.

TIP

After you start exploring different Web pages, you can start clicking the Back button to the left of the address bar to return to any of the previously viewed pages. Each time you click Back (or press Alt+←), Internet Explorer goes back to the very last page you viewed. If you've visited several pages during the same browsing session, you can jump to a particular page that you viewed by clicking the Recent Pages drop-down button that appears to the immediate right of the Forward button and then choosing the page you want to revisit from the drop-down list that appears.

You can clear the list of recently browsed Web pages at any time by clicking Safety⟹Delete Browsing History or pressing Ctrl+Shift+Del. Windows then opens the Delete Browsing History dialog box, where the Temporary Internet Files, Cookies, and History check boxes are automatically selected for elimination as soon as you click the dialog box's Delete button.

You can also revisit the list of pages that are in the browser's history (that is, the pages you've visited in the last 20 days unless you've changed the History option) by clicking the address bar's drop-down button. At that point, you can choose the URL of the page you want to revisit from the drop-down list that appears.

After using the Back button to revisit one or more previously viewed pages, the Forward button (right next door) becomes active. Click the Forward button (or press Alt+→) to step forward through each of the pages that you've viewed with the Back button, or select a page to jump to from the Forward button drop-down list.

If you come upon a page that doesn't seem to want to load for some reason (perhaps due to a broken hyperlink or too much Web traffic), click the Stop button (the one with the red X to the immediate left of the Bing Search text box) or press Esc to stop the process; then select a new Web site to visit. When revisiting a page, you can make sure that the content currently displayed by Internet Explorer is completely up-to-date by clicking the Refresh button (the one with the two arrows pointing down and up to the immediate left of the Stop Loading button).

Accelerators

Internet Explorer 8 supports a new feature called *accelerators*. Accelerators comprise a bunch of Internet Explorer 8–compatible add-ins that can make browsing some Web pages a whole lot more productive by giving you needed additional information on the spot without requiring a whole bunch more browsing. When Internet Explorer 8 is first installed, the program includes a number of accelerators (such as Map with Bing and Search with Bing) to which you can readily add others.

The most common accelerators include calling up an online dictionary so you can look up the definition of a selected term, searching for a term on the Web, or displaying an online map for an address right on the page containing the text. For example, Internet Explorer 8 comes with a Map with Bing accelerator already installed that you can use to display a mini-map for an address you've selected on the current Web page. Internet Explorer 8 also has a Search with Bing accelerator that you can use to do a Web search for any term you select.

Figure 4-3 shows you the Map with Bing accelerator in action. Here, I'm using this accelerator to display a mini-map of the nearest Macy's store, whose address I selected on the Store Locator & Hours Web page. To use this accelerator on this page, I simply selected the address listed on the page (by dragging the hand-pointing mouse cursor through the text). When you release the mouse button, a little blue accelerator menu button appears (with an icon of an arrow pointing up and to the right).

When you click this accelerator menu button, a pull-down menu showing all originally installed accelerators is displayed beneath it. (For a full list of all installed accelerators, highlight the All Accelerators item at the bottom.) You would then highlight the Map with Bing item on this pull-down menu to have this accelerator look up the selected address and display its location on the Bing mini-map that automatically pops up to the left of Map with Bing.

You can find and download additional accelerators from the Microsoft's Add-Ons Gallery. Simply highlight the All Accelerators item at the bottom of any accelerator pull-down menu and then click the Find More Accelerators item near the bottom of the continuation menu. Internet Explorer 8 then opens the Accelerators Add-Ons Gallery Web page containing a bunch of cool accelerators that you can download and install for use with IE 8.

If you're like me and often want to know the definitions of terms that you run across on the Web, be sure to download the Google Define accelerator from the Accelerators Add-Ons Gallery Web page. This nifty little add-on makes it possible to look up the definition and sites for any term that you select on the Web page you're visiting using Google's excellent search engine.

Address AutoComplete

Of all the methods for browsing pages on the Web, none is quite as bad as having to type Web addresses with the **http://** and the **www.*somethingorother*.com** in the address bar. To help eliminate errors in typing and speed this tedious process, Windows employs a feature called AutoComplete. This nifty tool looks at the first few characters of the URL you type in the address bar and, based on that, attempts to match them to one of the complete addresses that's stored in the address bar drop-down list.

For example, if you click in the address bar, select all the characters in the current Web address that follow http://www. (the standard beginning for most Web addresses), and then replace the last part of the current address with the letter *h,* AutoComplete opens the address bar drop-down list, displaying all the Web sites that you've visited recently whose URL (after the standard http://www. stuff) begins with *h.*

To visit any one of the Web addresses listed in the address bar drop-down list, simply click that Web address. Internet Explorer then enters the complete URL of the Web site you clicked in the address bar and automatically displays the page.

Figure 4-3

The AutoComplete feature also works when you browse folders on a local or network disk. To display a list of recently viewed documents on your hard drive, click in the address bar and then type the letter of your hard drive (**c**, in most cases); next, click the document you want to open in the address bar drop-down list.

Compatibility View

Internet Explorer 8 contains a new Compatibility View feature that enables this version of the browser to switch to a view when visiting Web sites that were created for older versions of Web browsers. By switching to this view, you can often fix alignment and spacing problems and enhance the look of the text on the pages of the Web site. Internet Explorer 8 lets you know when a particular Web site might benefit from Compatibility View by automatically displaying a Compatibility View button (with a torn page icon) in between the address bar and the Refresh button (the one with the two alternating arrows icon).

When you click the Compatibility View button (or choose the Compatibility View item from the Tools menu), IE 8 redraws the current page in the browser window in a way that conforms more with the standards of older browsers, then highlights the Compatibility View button next to the address bar and briefly displays a message beneath its Web tab, indicating that you're now viewing the site in Compatibility View.

InPrivate browsing

Internet Explorer 8 introduces a new way of browsing the Web referred to as InPrivate browsing. When you turn on InPrivate browsing and then visit a bunch of Web pages, Internet Explorer 8 doesn't leave a trail of the sites you browse in the program's History log and elsewhere on your computer. When you browse sites in this mode, Internet Explorer 8 doesn't save cookies (those bits of information about you and your user preferences such as logons that the Web site can use to identify you), doesn't save temporary Internet files, and doesn't save the Web addresses in the program's history log.

You can use InPrivate browsing whenever you don't want to leave a trail on the computer that other users can readily follow to see where you went. This feature comes in really handy when you're planning something special (such as a Caribbean getaway) for someone who also uses your computer and you don't want him or her to be able to look into the Web browser's history, thus spoiling the surprise.

Don't, however, use InPrivate Browsing when there's any chance that you may later need to retrace your steps on the Internet to relocate information you've already looked up. Remember that you can always manually purge the cookies, temporary Internet files, and history in Internet Explorer 8 by pressing Ctrl+Shift+Delete and then clicking the Delete button in the Delete Browsing History dialog box.

To browse the Web using the InPrivate Browsing feature, choose the InPrivate Browsing item from the Safety pull-down menu in IE 8 or press (Ctrl+Shift+P). Internet Explorer 8 then opens a new browsing window like the one shown in Figure 4-4. As you can see, this IE window displays a page with general information about InPrivate Browsing but more importantly displays an InPrivate button to the immediate left of the address bar. As long as this InPrivate button appears in front of the address bar, you know that the pages you visit are *not* being adding to the program's history log and that the browser isn't caching any of the temporary files that are downloaded as part of the a particular Web page display.

Keep in mind that there's no way to turn off InPrivate Browsing other than closing all the Internet Explorer 8 browser windows that contain the InPrivate button and then surfing Web pages in the original Internet Explorer 8 window that doesn't bear this button. (Clicking the InPrivate button itself in a browser window only serves to display a pop-up menu telling you that InPrivate Browsing is currently turned on — something you were probably already well aware of.)

Figure 4-4

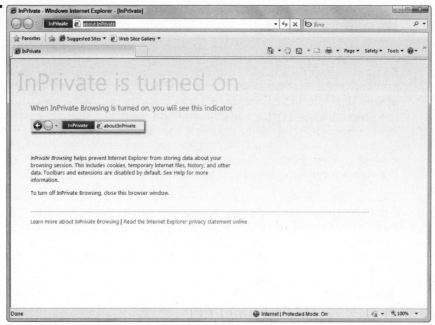

Web slices

Another really nifty feature in Internet Explorer 8 is called *Web slices*. Web slices keep an eye on particular information that's constantly being updated so that you don't have to continually revisit the site that contains the changing information in order to be up-to-date on it. The most obvious use for Web slices are items that you bid on or want to bid on in eBay auctions. By adding the particular items you're interested in winning as a Web slice, you can keep your eye on the bids that come as the auction deadline nears in Internet Explorer 8 without having to actually return to the item's page on the eBay Web site.

Figures 4-5 and 4-6 show you how Web slices work in IE 8. For Figure 4-5, I visited eBay with IE and then did a search on the site for auctions of retro table lamps. Then, as I positioned the mouse over various lamps that were up for auction, a little green Web slice button appeared to the immediate left of each description. After locating a vintage, mid-century, Eames-era lamp that I wanted to bid on in the list, I clicked its green button and Internet Explorer 8 displays the Add a Web Slice dialog box that you also see in this figure.

Figure 4-5

After clicking the Add to Favorites Bar button in the Add a Web Slice dialog box, the Internet Explorer adds a button for the vintage lamp at the start of the Favorites bar, as shown in Figure 4-6. From then on, I can always get information on the number of bids and the time remaining till the lamp's eBay auction ends by clicking this button on the Favorites bar even when I'm surfing other Web sites and am nowhere near eBay. After the auction is over (and I've won the lamp), I can remove the button from the Favorites bar by right-clicking it and then choosing Delete from its shortcut menu.

Zooming in on a page

If the text on the Web page you're visiting is too small for you to read comfortably on your screen, click the 100% button on the Status bar in the bottom-right corner of the Internet Explorer 8 window to zoom in on the page: Click once to zoom up to 125% magnification and click a second time to zoom up to a 150% magnification. Clicking this button a third time returns you to 100%. Note that you can also zoom in by using the keyboard and pressing the Ctrl key and the plus key (+).

Figure 4-6

If you need to boost the magnification of a Web page beyond 150%, you can select the percentage from the Zoom drop-down menu, which you access by positioning the mouse pointer over (or clicking) the Page drop-down button (to the immediate left of Safety on the toolbar) and then highlighting or clicking Zoom. The Zoom menu percentage selections include 50%, 75%, 100%, 125%, 150%, 200%, 400%, and Custom. You can also do zoom by clicking the Change Zoom Level button (the drop-down button to the immediate right of the 100% button on the Status bar) and clicking the percentage item from its pop-up menu.

If none of these presets work for you, click Custom to open the Custom Zoom dialog box, where you can type any whole percentage number between 1 and 1,000 in the Percentage Zoom text box, or select it with the up and down spinner buttons before you click OK.

You can also use the shortcut keys Ctrl+plus sign (+) and Ctrl+minus sign (–) to zoom the Web page up and down, respectively, in 10% increments.

Bookmarking Web sites as favorites

You keep bookmarks for all of your preferred Web pages for easy revisiting. You can access these bookmarks (also known as *favorites*) from the Favorites/Feeds/History Explorer bar containing three tabs: Favorites, Feeds, and History. To open this bar, you click the View Favorites, Feeds, and History button (simply labeled Favorites) that appears at the very beginning of the Favorite toolbar at the top of the Internet Explorer window (or you can simply press Alt+C).

 If you display the Classic menus in Internet Explorer 8 (by choosing Tools⊏> Toolbars⊏>Menu Bar), you can access links to your bookmarked Web pages directly from the Favorites drop-down menu.

When you first start adding bookmarks to the Favorites tab of the Favorites/ Feeds/History bar, you'll find that it already contains folders such as Microsoft Websites, MSN Websites, and Windows Live. In addition, the Favorites folder may contain a folder with your computer manufacturer's favorite Web sites (called something like "XYZ" Corporation Recommended Sites), Mobile Favorites (if you connect a hand-held device to the computer), and a folder called Imported Bookmarks, if you imported bookmarks created in another Web browser that you use on your computer.

When you start adding Web favorite buttons to the Favorites toolbar (the bar that appears right beneath the row with the address bar), you find that it already contains Suggested Sites and Get More Add-ons buttons. Click the Suggested Sites button on the Favorites toolbar and then click the Turn on Suggested Sites button in its drop-down menu to have IE 8 use your browsing history to suggest similar sites that you might also want to surf. Click the Get More Add-ons button and then click the Find More in the Internet Explorer Add-ons Gallery link in its drop-down menu to open the Microsoft Internet Explorer 8 Add-ons Gallery Web page on a new tab in your browser, where you can down-load accelerators and Web slices for the browser.

Adding bookmarks to the Favorites toolbar

If you plan to regularly visit the Web site you're bookmarking, you may want to add its bookmark as a button on the Internet Explorer 8's Favorites toolbar. That way, you don't even have to bother with opening the Favorites/Feeds/ History Explorer bar or the Favorites pull-down menu in order to revisit the site.

To add a favorite Web site as a button on the Favorites toolbar, you follow these two simple steps:

1. First launch Internet Explorer 8 (by clicking the Internet Explorer Quick Launch button on the Windows taskbar) and then browse to the Web page you want to add to the Favorites toolbar.

2. Click the toolbar's Add to Favorites Bar button (the one with only the star-with-the-plus-sign icon and no label) that appears to the immediate right of the View Favorites, Feeds, History button (labeled Favorites) at the very beginning of the Favorites toolbar.

Internet Explorer 8 then adds a button for that Web page to the beginning of the Favorites toolbar — to the immediate right of the Add to Favorites Bar button. You can then click this toolbar button anytime you want to display the Web site in the current tab of the browser.

Adding bookmarks to the Favorites/Feeds/History (Explorer) bar

To bookmark a favorite Web site and add it to your Favorites/Feeds/History bar and Favorites pull-down menu, follow these steps:

1. First launch Internet Explorer 8 and then browse to the Web page you'd like to bookmark.

   See "Browsing the Web" earlier in this part for details on how to open a Web page.

2. Click the Visit Favorites, Feeds, and History button (marked Favorites on the Favorites toolbar) to open the Favorites tab of the Favorites/Feeds/History bar and then click its Add to Favorites button (which has an icon of a star with a plus sign) at the top of the bar or press Ctrl+D to open the Add a Favorite dialog box, which looks similar to the one shown in Figure 4-7.

   You can also open the Add a Favorite dialog box by right-clicking anywhere on the Web page itself and then choosing Add to Favorites from the shortcut menu that appears.

3. (Optional) If you want a different description to appear on the Favorites menu, edit the name that currently appears in the Name text box.

4. (Optional) To add the bookmark to a subfolder of the Favorites folder, click the Create In drop-down menu to display a list of subfolders and then click the icon of the subfolder in which to add the bookmark. To add the bookmark to a new folder, click the New Folder button, enter the folder name in the Folder Name text box of the Create a Folder dialog box, and then click Create.

5. Click the Add button to close the Add a Favorite dialog box and add the bookmark to the Favorites tab on the Favorites/Feeds/History bar.

Opening favorites

After you add a Web page to your Favorites folder (or one of the subfolders), you can open the page simply by selecting the bookmark, either from the Favorites tab on the Favorites/Feeds/History bar or from the Favorites pull-down menu (if the Classic menus are displayed; press Alt+A if the menus are hidden).

To open the list of your IE 8 bookmarks on the Favorites tab of the Favorites/Feeds/History bar, click the View Favorites, Feeds, and History button on the Favorites toolbar or press Alt+C. To visit a favorite listed in the tab, click its link. The Internet Explorer then opens the page in the browser window, while at the same time closing the Favorites/Feeds/History Explorer bar. If the bookmark you want to visit is saved in a subfolder, click that folder's icon on the bar's Favorites tab to expand and display a list of the favorite links it contains, which you can click to display the page.

View Favorites, Feeds and History button

Figure 4-7

 You can keep the Favorites/Feeds/History Explorer bar open either by pressing Ctrl+Shift+I or by clicking the Pin the Favorites Center button (the one with the green arrow pointing to the left in the Explorer bar's right corner). When you want to close the Favorites/Feeds/History bar, press Ctrl+Shift+I again or click the Close button (the one with the X).

 To select a bookmarked Web site from the Favorites pull-down menu when the Classic menus are displayed in Internet Explorer, choose Favorites from the menu bar and then select the name of the bookmark on the menu. If the bookmark is located in a subfolder of Favorites, you need to drill down to the subfolder icon to open the submenu, where you can click the desired bookmark.

Organizing favorites

Many times, you'll find yourself going along adding bunches of bookmarks for your preferred Web pages without ever bothering to place them in particular subfolders. Then, to your dismay, you'll find yourself confronted with a seemingly endless list of unrelated bookmarks every time you open the Favorites/Feeds/History bar or Favorites pull-down menu.

Fortunately, Windows makes it easy to reorganize even the most chaotic of bookmark lists in just a few easy steps:

1. In Internet Explorer 8, click the View Favorites, Feeds, and History button and then click the Add to Favorites button (with the plus sign) at the top of the Favorites/Feeds/History Explorer bar or press Alt+Z and then click Organize Favorites on the drop-down menu to open the Organize Favorites dialog box.

   The list box in the Organize Favorites dialog box shows all the subfolders, followed by all the bookmarks in the Favorites folder (similar to the one shown in Figure 4-8).

Figure 4-8

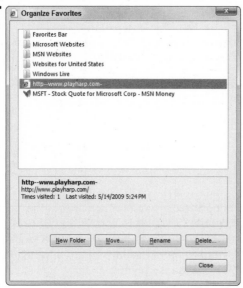

2. To move a bookmark into one of the subfolders, drag its icon and then drop it on the icon of the subfolder. Alternatively, click the favorite to select it and then click the Move button to open the Browse for Folder dialog box. Then click the destination folder in the Browse for Folder dialog box and click OK.

Use the following options in the Organize Favorites dialog box to create new folders to hold your bookmarks, to rename bookmarks, or even to get rid of unwanted bookmarks:

✔ **To create a new folder,** click the New Folder button; then type a new name for the folder and press Enter.

✔ **To rename a link to a favorite Web page,** click the icon to select it, click the Rename button, edit the item name, and then press Enter.

✔ **To delete a link to a favorite Web page,** click the icon and then click the Delete button. Click Yes in the Delete File dialog box when it asks whether you're sure that you want to send that particular favorite to the Recycle Bin.

 You can also use the drag-and-drop method to reorder the bookmarks on the Favorites tab of the Favorites/Feeds/History Explorer bar (Ctrl+Shift+I), as follows:

✔ To open one of the folders on the Favorites/Feeds/History bar to display the folder contents, click the folder icon. Internet Explorer then displays a series of icons for each of the subfolders and bookmarks its contents. To close a folder to hide the contents, click the folder icon again.

✔ To move a bookmark to a new position in the folder, drag that icon up or down until you reach the desired position. As you drag, you see where the item will be inserted by the appearance of a heavy, horizontal I-beam between the bookmarks. You also see where you *cannot* move the icon because of the display of the international no-no symbol.

✔ To move a bookmark icon to a different (existing) folder, drag the book-mark icon to the folder icon. When the folder icon is highlighted, you can drop the favorite icon into it.

Using Internet Explorer 8 tabs

Internet Explorer 8 displays each Web page that you browse in a tab showing the page name. This current tab isn't the only one you can have in the Internet Explorer window. To add a tab to the Internet Explorer, click the New Tab button (the blank button to the immediate right of the current tab in which a page icon appears as soon as you position the mouse pointer on it) or press Ctrl+T.

When you click the New Tab button or press Ctrl+T key, Internet Explorer adds a What Do You Want to Do Next Web page in a new tab that appears to the right of the tab for the page you were viewing. The program also inserts a Quick Tabs button (the one with four buttons arranged in a square) to the immediate left of the first Web tab.

When you navigate to another Web page after adding a new tab, Internet Explorer displays that page and enters its title in the new tab. You can then go back and forth between the Web page that's open in the first tab and the one you just navigated to in the new tab by clicking their tabs.

You can also switch between open pages by clicking the Quick Tabs button or pressing Ctrl+Q to display thumbnails of all the pages open on different tabs (see Figure 4-9). Finally, click the thumbnail of the page you want to display in the current tab.

Click the Quick Tabs button or press Ctrl+Q a second time to close the Quick Tabs view and return to the normal page display in Internet Explorer 8. You can also click the drop-down button to the immediate right of the Quick Tabs button to display a list of all the tabs you have open in Internet Explorer (helpful when you have so many tabs open that you can no longer easily read the names of their pages on the tab bar). To select a new tab and display a new Web page, you simply click its name on this drop-down list.

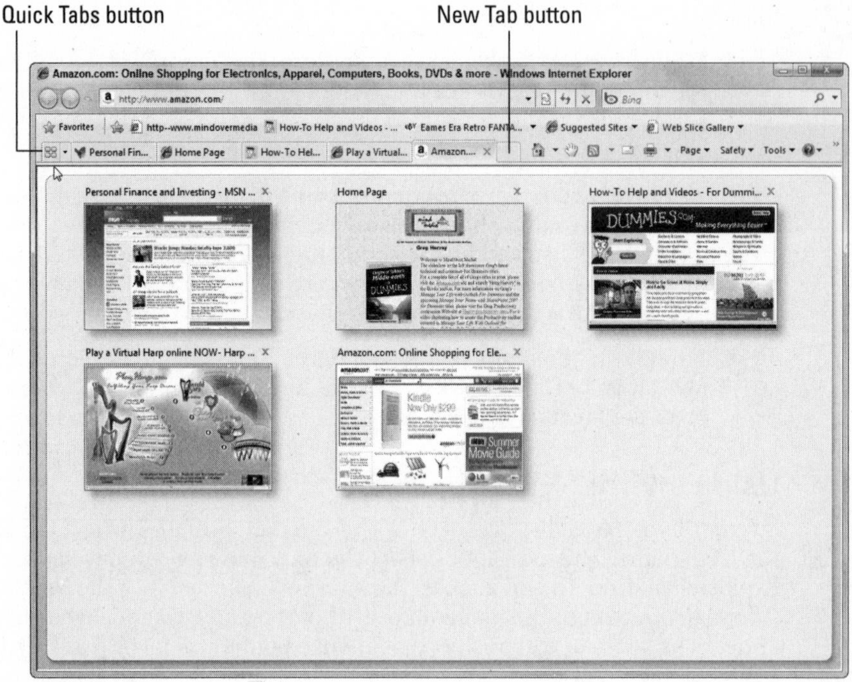

Quick Tabs button   New Tab button

Figure 4-9

Note that you can close the tab for an open page in the Quick Tabs view by clicking the close button (the one with the black X) that appears in the upper-right corner of the title bar of its thumbnail image (opposite the page title). You can also close a tab by clicking the close button that appears to the immediate right of the current page's tab when Internet Explorer is not in Quick Tabs view.

When you exit IE 8 after creating a bunch of tabs for the different Web pages you've been visiting, the program displays an alert dialog box asking whether you want to close all the tabs (which you must do by clicking its Close All Tabs button in order to shut down Internet Explorer). If all you want to do is close the Web page displayed in the current tab of the browser, click the Close Current Tab button instead.

Saving Web graphics

As you're browsing Web pages with Internet Explorer, you may come upon some sites that offer graphics or other images for downloading. You have a few choices when it comes to saving Web graphics on your computer hard drive. You can save images

- ✔ **As a graphic file** for viewing and printing in the Pictures library by right-clicking the image and then choosing Save Picture As from the shortcut menu that appears.

- ✔ **As the wallpaper for your desktop** by right-clicking the graphic and then clicking Set as Background from its shortcut menu. Click the Yes button in the alert dialog box that appears asking whether you're sure you want to replace the current background.

 Keep in mind that when you save a Web graphic as the wallpaper for your desktop, Windows 7 uses its Fill option to stretch the picture so that it fills the entire desktop (which most often results in a severely distorted image). To center it in the middle of the desktop or to tile the image (by duplicating it across the entire desktop), right-click the desktop, choose Personalize from its shortcut menu, and then click the Desktop Background link. Click the Center or Tile option button under How Should the Picture Be Positioned before you click OK.

 You can also save a graphic on a Web page as an attachment in a new e-mail that you can then send to a friend or colleague. To perform this trick, right-click the image and then choose the E-Mail Picture option from the shortcut menu that appears. An Internet Explorer Security alert dialog may then appear, asking your permission to open the Web content on your computer; just click the Allow button to continue. Windows then opens an Attach Files dialog box that shows the current size of the image and enables you to select a more or less compressed version to send by choosing its new size from the Picture Size drop-down list. After selecting the size, click the Attach button to open a new message in your e-mail program that you can then address and send.

Saving Web pages

Occasionally, you may want to save an entire Web page on your computer (text, hyperlinks, graphics, and all). To save the Web page that currently appears in Internet Explorer 8, click the Page drop-down button on the Command toolbar and then choose Save As from its drop-down menu to open the Save Webpage dialog box. In this dialog box, you can select the folder in which to save the page, assign a filename to it, and even change its file type.

 If the Classic menus are displayed in Internet Explorer 8, you can also open the Save Webpage dialog box by choosing File➪Save As. If the menus are not displayed, you can press Alt+FA to open the Save Webpage dialog box.

By default, Internet Explorer saves the Web pages as a Web Archive file with a .mht file extension that this browser can read. However, you can select one of these other options from the Save as Type drop-down list if you want:

- ✔ If you want to save all the text and graphics on the page as a full-fledged HTML file that any Web browser and many other programs can open, select the Webpage, Complete (*.htm, *html) option.

- ✔ If you're only concerned about having the text on the page saved in HTML, select the Webpage, HTML only (*.htm, *html) option.

- ✔ If you want to be able to use the text on the Web page in any Word processor or with any text editor, select the Text File (*.txt) option.

After you make your selection, click the Save button.

After saving a Web page as an HTML file on your hard drive, you can open it in Internet Explorer and view the contents even when you're not connected to the Internet. If your motive for saving the Web page, however, is to be able to view the content when you're not connected to the Internet, you're better off saving the page as a favorite marked for offline viewing. That way, you can decide whether you want to view other pages linked to the one you're saving, and you can have Internet Explorer check the site for updated content when your computer eventually does have Internet access.

You can also e-mail a Web page in the body of a new e-mail message by clicking the Page button and then choosing the Send Page by E-mail option from the drop-down menu. Windows 7 then opens an Internet Explorer Security dialog box where you click the Allow button. After that, a new e-mail opens in your computer's e-mail program that you can address and send. (If you don't have an e-mail program installed on your computer, select the E-mail with Windows Live item on this pull-down menu to go online where you can use your Hotmail account to send the page in a new e-mail via the Internet.)

When visiting a complex Web site with loads of graphics, you may not want to take the time to send an entire page from the site in an e-mail. Instead, send a link to the page by clicking the Page button and then clicking Send Link by E-mail to open a new message with your e-mail program containing a link to the page in the body of the message and the name of the page in the Subject field.

Printing Web pages

When browsing Web pages in Internet Explorer 8, you may come across a page you'd like print out. Internet Explorer 8 not only makes it easy to print the Web pages you go to see, but also gives you the ability to preview the printout before you commit your printer.

To preview the current Web page, click the drop-down button attached to the Printer button on the tab row (don't click the Print button itself because doing so opens the Print dialog box rather than the Print Preview window) and then choose Print Preview from its drop-down menu. Windows then opens the first printed page for the Web page you're printing in a Print Preview window, similar to the one shown in Figure 4-10.

Figure 4-10

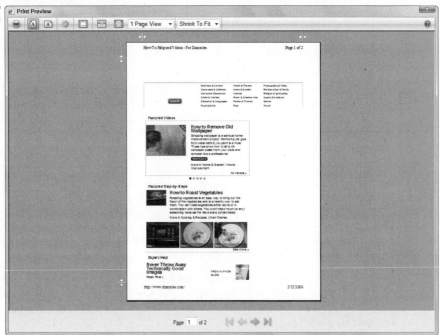

If the Classic menus are displayed in Internet Explorer, you can also open the Print Preview window by choosing File⇨Print Preview.

The Print Preview toolbar at the top of this window contains some important buttons for modifying the view of the pages in the preview window:

- ✔ **Print Document (Alt+P)** prints the Web page(s) previewed in the Print Preview window using whatever settings are current.

- ✔ **Portrait (Alt+O)** displays the printed page in portrait mode, which prints text across the shorter edge of the paper in lines running down the longer edge.

- ✔ **Landscape (Alt+L)** displays the page in landscape mode, which prints text across the longer edge of the paper in lines running down the shorter edge.

- ✔ **Page Setup (Alt+U)** opens the Page Setup dialog box, where you can change paper size and source, add a header and footer for the printout and specify the top, bottom, left, and right margins.

✔ **Turn Headers and Footers On and Off (Alt+E)** turns off and on the display of any headers and/or footers you specify for the printout in the Page Setup dialog box.

✔ **View Full Width (Alt+W)** adjusts the magnification of the current page so that it fills the full width of the Print Preview window.

✔ **View Full Page (Alt+1)** adjusts the magnification of the page preview so that the full length of the current page fits within the Print Preview window.

✔ **Show Multiple Pages (Alt+N)** switches among 1-Page View (the default), 2-Page View, 3-Page View, 6-Page View, and 12-Page View settings that determine the number of pages (displayed in the Print Preview window) over which Internet Explorer spreads the printed contents of the current Web page.

✔ **Change Print Size (Alt+S)** stretches or shrinks the printout of the pages a particular percentage of its actual size (between 30% and 200% or a Custom setting). Alternatively, you can use the Shrink To Fit default setting to have Internet Explorer automatically make all the content fit on the number of pages selected in the Show Multiple Pages drop-down list.

✔ **Help (F1)** opens a Microsoft Internet Explorer Help window with information on using Print Preview.

The status bar at the bottom of the window contains the following controls for displaying different pages of the printout in the Print Preview window (when the default 1-Page View Show Multiple Pages setting is selected) and sending the printout to the printer:

✔ **Current Page (Alt+A)** selects the text box that displays the number of the current page. Type another page number in this text box and press Enter to display that page of the preview.

✔ **First Page (Alt+Home)** displays the first page of the preview.

✔ **Previous Page (Alt+Left Arrow)** displays the previous page of the preview.

✔ **Next Page (Alt+Right Arrow)** displays the next page of the preview.

✔ **Last Page (Alt+End)** displays the last page of the preview.

To close the Print Preview window and return to the current Web page without printing the page, click the Close button (the red one with the X) in the upper-right corner of the Print Preview window.

If you choose not to print from the Print Preview window or you're sure that you don't need to use Print Preview to get the information you want, you can print the Web page currently displayed in Internet Explorer by clicking the Print option on the Page drop-down list or by pressing Ctrl+P to open the Print dialog box. In this dialog box, you can specify such options as the printer name, pages to print, and number of copies. When you're ready, click the Print button to send the pages to the printer.

Working offline

To facilitate the use of RSS feeds (*see* "Subscribing to RSS Feeds" later in this part) and Web page subscriptions, Internet Explorer 8 supports offline browsing (as opposed to online browsing, which indicates being connected to the Internet). Offline browsing is especially beneficial when you're using a laptop computer and can't get connected to the Internet (as when in transit on a bus, train, or plane). It can also come in handy when you rely on a relatively slow dialup connection to the Internet (as with 28.8 or 33.3 Kbps modems), enabling you to download Web content during nonpeak hours and browse it with maximum efficiency during the peak surfing hours (thereby totally avoiding the "World Wide Wait").

To turn offline browsing on and off, choose Work Offline from the Tools drop-down menu (or you can choose File⇨Work Offline if the Classic menus are displayed or press Alt+FW when they're hidden). Note that after you put the browsing window in offline mode, if you don't manually go back online, the browser remains in this work mode until you restart your computer. In other words, if you shut down the browsing window and then relaunch it during the same work session in Windows, the browser opens in offline mode. If you decide that you want to do some serious online surfing during that same session, you need to manually start by choosing Tools⇨Work Offline to turn off the offline mode.

When offline mode is on (indicated by a check mark in front of the Work Offline command on the Tools drop-down menu), Windows won't automatically attempt to connect to the Internet, and you can browse only pages stored locally on your computer, such as those that have been downloaded into the *cache* on your computer hard drive. Also known as the temporary Internet files, the cache contains all Web pages and their components that are downloaded when you subscribe to Web sites or channels.

When you browse a Web site offline from a local drive, you have none of the wait often associated with browsing online when connected to the Internet. You may also find, however, that some of the links aren't available for offline viewing. Internet Explorer lets you know when a link isn't available by adding the international "No" or "Don't" symbol (you know, the circle with a backslash in it) to the normal hand mouse pointer.

If you persist and click a hyperlink to a page that hasn't been downloaded, the browsing window displays a Web Page Unavailable While Offline alert dialog box, indicating that the Web page you requested is not available for browsing. To have Internet Explorer connect you to the Internet and go to the requested page, click the Connect button or press Enter. To remain offline and close the alert dialog box, click the Stay Offline button instead.

Most of the time when browsing offline, you do your local Web surfing in one of two ways:

✔ **By visiting updated Web pages marked as Favorites that have been stored in the cache for later (offline) viewing.** You open these pages by selecting them from the Favorites/Feeds/History Explorer bar (opened by clicking the View Favorites, Feeds, and History button on the Favorites toolbar) or by choosing them from the Favorites menu.

✔ **By revisiting Web pages stored in the cache as part of the History.** You open these pages by selecting them from the History Explorer bar, which you open by pressing Ctrl+Shift+H, by clicking the History tab on the Favorites/Feeds/History bar, or by choosing View➪Explorer Bars➪History from the Internet Explorer menu bar.

In addition to using these two browsing methods, you can open Web pages that are stored in folders on local disks, such as the hard drive or a CD-ROM in your CD-ROM drive. The easiest way to open these pages is by selecting the drive letter in the address bar of Internet Explorer. You can also open a local Web page with the Open dialog box (choose File➪Open when the Classic menus are displayed or press Ctrl+O).

Searching from the Bing Search text box

The World Wide Web holds an enormous wealth of information on almost every subject known to humanity — and it's of absolutely no use if you don't know how to get to it. To help Web surfers such as yourself locate the sites containing the information you need, a number of so-called *search engines* have been designed. Each search engine maintains a slightly different directory of the sites on the World Wide Web (which are mostly maintained and updated by auto-mated programs called by such wonderfully suggestive names as Web crawlers, spiders, and robots!). Internet Explorer 8 uses its new Bing Search engine to find your next new favorite Web sites.

Internet Explorer 8 makes it easy to search the World Wide Web from the Bing Search text box located to the immediate right of the Stop button on the bar containing the address bar. After you click the text box and then enter the key-word or words (known affectionately as a *search string,* in programmer's par-lance) to search for in this text box, you begin the search by clicking the Search button (the one with the magnifying glass) or by pressing Enter.

Bing Search also helps you find sites of interest by displaying possible topics in a list on a drop-down menu whose names start with the characters that you type as the search string. If the topic you want to search appears on this list, you can begin the Web search by clicking its name on the menu.

If you want the search results page to appear in a new tab rather than replace the Web page displayed in the current tab, press Alt+Enter after entering your search string into the Bing Search text box.

Internet Explorer 8 conducts a search for Web sites containing the keywords you entered and then displays the first page of matching results. To visit one of the sites in this list, click its hyperlink. To view the next page of Web search results (assuming that you get more than one page of matches, which is usually the case), click the number of the next page or the Next hyperlink at the bottom of the Bing Search page. To go back to the search results page after having visited one of the Web pages listed, click the Back button or press Alt+←.

After you're convinced that you've seen the best matches to your search, but you still haven't found the Web site(s) you're looking for, you can conduct another search in the Bing Search text box by using slightly different terms.

To search for particular information on the Web site you're visiting (as opposed to finding a page on the World Wide Web), click the drop-down button to the immediate right of the Search button and then choose Find on This Page from its drop-down menu. Internet Explorer opens a Find dialog box, where you can enter your search text (in the Find text box), specify whether to match whole words only, upper- or lowercase, and the search direction and then start the search by clicking its Next or Previous button.

Autosearching from the address bar

In addition to searching from the Bing Search text box, Internet Explorer 8 enables you to perform searches from its address bar by using a feature referred to as Autosearching. To conduct an Autosearch from the address bar, you need to first click in the address bar (to select the current entry) and then preface the search string with one of the following three terms:

- ✔ Go
- ✔ Find
- ✔ ?

To search for Web sites whose descriptions contain the terms *Thai cuisine,* for example, you could type

```
go Thai food
```

or

```
find Thai food
```

or even

```
? Thai food
```

in the address bar. After you enter **go**, **find**, or **?** followed by the search string, press the Enter key to have Windows conduct the search.

When you press Enter, Internet Explorer opens the Bing Search page with the first 10 to 20 matches to your search string (depending upon your screen resolution).

Adding a search provider to Internet Explorer 8

Bing Search isn't the only search provider supported by Internet Explorer 8. If you're more confident using another provider such as Google or Yahoo!, you can add it to the Internet Explorer 8 browser and even make it — rather than Bing Search — the default search engine. Here's how:

1. Click the drop-down button to the immediate right of the Search button in the Bing Search text box and then choose Find More Providers from the button's drop-down menu.

   The program opens the Search Providers Add-Ons Gallery page in the Internet Explorer 8 window, similar to the one shown in Figure 4-11.

2. Click the Add to Internet Explorer button next to the name of the Web Search provider you want to add (Wikipedia Visual, Search, Yahoo! Search Suggestions, Google Search Suggestions, and so on).

   Windows displays an Add Search Provider dialog box asking whether you want to add the selected search provider to Internet Explorer.

3. (Optional) To make the selected search provider the default search engine that Internet Explorer first uses whenever you search the Web, select the Make This My Default Search Provider check box.

4. Click the Add Provider button to close the dialog box and add the provider.

To use the new search provider you've added to Internet Explorer 8, choose the provider's name from the Bing Search button's drop-down menu. As soon as you do so, the provider's logo appears at the very beginning of the erstwhile Bing Search text box, as in the black W icon for Wikipedia Visual Search and the blue, red, yellow, and green background that defines a white G for Google Search Suggestions.

You can also use this four-step procedure to add topical search engines to Internet Explorer 8 such as New York Times Instant Search, Amazon Search Suggestions, eBay Visual Search, and ESPN Search.

Keep in mind that after you follow this procedure to add Web and topical search providers to Internet Explorer 8, their names then appear (in alphabetical order) on the Bing Search drop-down menu. You can then select a new search provider on-the-fly simply by clicking the provider's name on this drop-down menu before you conduct a search that would use its particular body of knowledge or products. For example, to quickly find my page on Amazon.com, you'd enter **greg harvey** in Internet Explorer's Bing Search text box and then select Amazon Visual Search (assuming that you've already added it to Internet Explorer 8) from the Bing Search drop-down menu.

Figure 4-11

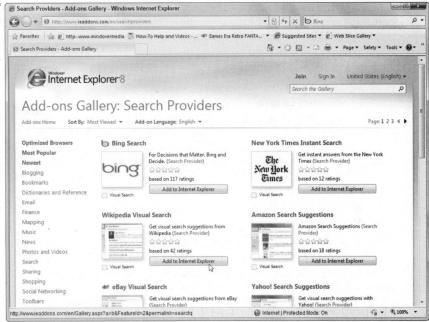

No phishing allowed

Phishing (and, no that's not a misspelling) refers to a very special kind of illegal fishing on the Internet, whereby someone fraudulently poses as a legitimate business entity in order to get you to pony up some very private and sensitive information, such as your Social Security number, passwords, and/or credit card numbers, which, if he obtains, he puts to no good use (at least as far as you're concerned).

The damage caused by phishing can run the gamut from a simple inability to access your e-mail all the way to some pretty heavy financial losses. To help you guard against this kind of identity theft, Internet Explorer 8 includes a SmartScreen Filter feature that automatically checks each site you visit to determine whether it might possibly just be somebody's big old phishing hole, rather than a legitimate business with whom you can share sensitive information with a modicum of confidence.

If you visit a Web page that's on Microsoft's list of phishing Web sites, Internet Explorer displays a warning Web page and notification on the address bar. You can then continue to browse the site or close it from the warning Web page. If you visit a Web page that is not on this list but which exhibits suspicious characteristics, Internet Explorer only warns you that the site *might* be a phishing site on the address bar.

If you become suspicious of a particular Web site that you've never visited before, you can have Internet Explorer 8 check the site by choosing Safety➪ SmartScreen Filter➪Check This Website from the toolbar menu. A SmartScreen Filter alert dialog box then appears, telling you that the current Web site address will be sent to Microsoft to check against a list of known phishing sites. Click OK.

If you're more than a little suspicious of a particular site, you can submit a report to Microsoft indicating that you think this is a phishing site (so that it can check out the site and, if it proves to be fishy, redline it for other Internet Explorer 8 users) by choosing Tools➪SmartScreen Filter➪Report Unsafe Website from the toolbar menu. Click the Submit button in the Feedback – Windows Internet Explorer window after selecting the I Think This Is a Phishing Website check box and/or I Think this Website Contains Malicious Software.

Pop-ups anyone?

Perhaps one of the most annoying aspects of browsing the World Wide Web is coming across those pages littered with awful automated pop-up ads. (You know, the ones that appear the moment you load the page, with ads offering you all sorts of unusable stuff and unreal opportunities.) Fortunately, Internet Explorer 8 comes equipped with a Pop-Up Blocker feature — turned on by default — that prevents the display of any automated pop-ups on a page that want to magically materialize the moment you load the page.

Internet Explorer lets you know that it has blocked a pop-up on a page by displaying a message to that effect at the top of the page. To go ahead and display an automated pop-up, you then click Show Blocked Pop-up.

If you have a favorite Web site whose automated pop-ups you want to see, you can add that site's Web address to a list of exceptions in the Pop-up Blocker Settings dialog box (opened by choosing Tools➪Pop-Up Blocker➪Pop-Up Blocker Settings from the toolbar menu).

 By default, Windows 7 sets the Pop-Up Blocker to Medium: Block Most Automatic Pop-Ups setting, meaning that all automated pop-ups on a page that are not on the Trusted sites list (*see* Part 5) are blocked. If you really, really hate pop-ups, you can block them even on a trusted Web site by clicking the High: Block All Pop-Ups (Ctrl+Alt to Override) option on the Filter Level drop-down list in the Pop-Up Blocker Settings dialog box.

Subscribing to RSS feeds

Internet Explorer 8 supports *RSS feeds* (RSS either stands for Really Simple Syndication or Rich Site Summary, depending upon whom you ask). RSS feeds typically provide summaries of particular types of Web content that you're interested in keeping up-to-date on, although they may occasionally include full text and even some multimedia attachments.

RSS feeds are commonly used by news Web sites such as Reuters, CNN, NPR, and the BBC to feed their syndicated headlines to the users who subscribe to them. (Subscribers can then click particular headlines of interest to go to the page containing the full news story.) The feeds are also used by Weblog sites to keep their subscribers up-to-date as well as on the latest podcasts and vodcasts posted to such blogs.

TIP

RSS feeds are normally indicated on a Web page you're browsing by the words *Subscribe* or *Subscribe to This Feed,* or with an orange rectangle with radio waves emanating from a single point (same as the Feeds button on the IE 8 toolbar shown in most of the figures in this chapter) or with the letters *RSS* or *XML* in an orange rectangle. (Podcasts are often indicated by this same orange icon wearing headphones.) Of course, if you're interested in finding RSS news feeds to subscribe to, the easiest way to do this is by doing a Web search for RSS feeds or for a particular news organization. (**See** "Searching from the Live Search text box" earlier in this part for details.)

Internet Explorer 8 indicates that the Web page you're visiting contains RSS feeds by turning the Feeds button on the tab row to orange (so that it matches the color of the RSS rectangles on the page). Then, to subscribe to a particular RSS feed on that page, either click its RSS or podcast rectangle icon directly on the page or click the drop-down button attached to the Feeds button on the Internet Explorer 8 toolbar (located on the far right of the browser's Tab row) and then select the name of the feed in the drop-down menu.

After selecting the RSS feed in this manner, you can then subscribe to the feed by clicking the Subscribe or Subscribe to This Feed link on the Web page that lists the current headlines or Webcasts. You end up at a page like the one shown in Figure 4-12 (this particular figure shows you the feed for the NPR Topics: News Web page), where you can subscribe by clicking its Subscribe to This Feed link.

After you click a Subscribe or Subscribe to This Feed link, Internet Explorer opens a Subscribe to this Feed dialog box similar to the one shown in Figure 4-13. You can then change any of the following options in the alert dialog box before you click its Subscribe button to add this RSS feed to your Favorites Center:

  ✔ **Name:** Use this text box to modify the name automatically given to the feed by its Web site.

  ✔ **Create In:** Use this drop-down list to select a folder in the Favorites Center other than Feeds in which to add the RSS feed.

  ✔ **New Folder:** Use this button to create a new folder in the Favorites Center in which to save the RSS feed.

Figure 4-12

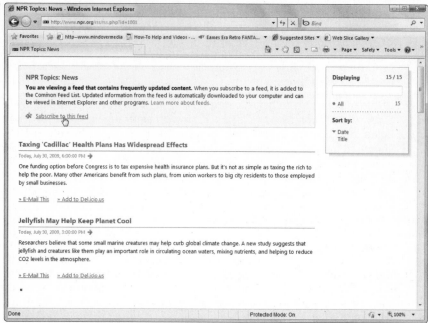

After you click the Subscribe button to close this alert dialog box, a message appears at the RSS Feed Web page, indicating that you've successfully subscribed to the Web feed and that you can access the RSS feed by clicking the View Feeds link. You can also do subscribe by opening the Favorites/Feeds/History Explorer bar (by clicking the View Favorites, Feeds, and History button on the Favorites toolbar), clicking the Feeds tab on this bar (or just pressing Ctrl+J), and then clicking the name of the feed in the Feeds Explorer bar that appears.

Figure 4-13

TIP

The easiest way to access an RSS feed is from the Feed Headlines gadget on the Windows 7 desktop. (*See* Part 1 for details on adding gadgets to the Windows desktop.) To select the RSS feed whose headlines you want displayed in this gadget, position the mouse pointer over the right edge of the Feed Headlines gadget and then click its wrench icon to display the Feed Headlines pop-up dialog box. Click the name of the RSS feed in the Display This Feed drop-down list and the number of headlines to display in the Number of Recent Headlines to Show drop-down list before you click OK.

Keep in mind that when you're visiting an RSS feed Web page to view its syndi- cated headlines or podcast listings, you access the news story or podcast in Internet Explorer 8 by clicking its link. To see the last time that Internet Explorer downloaded information from an RSS feed Web page, position the mouse pointer over the name of the Web page on the Feeds tab of the Favorites/Feeds/History bar to display this information in a ScreenTip.

Speech Recognition

The Speech Recognition feature in Windows 7 enables you to set up your com- puter to receive voice commands as well as to dictate text in applications such as Microsoft Word and Excel. In addition, you can configure the Text to Speech feature used to read aloud text in Windows 7 windows and dialog boxes when- ever you turn on the Narrator feature. (*See* "Ease of Access" in Part 5 for details.)

You can set up and fine-tune Speech Recognition by using the links in the Speech Recognition Control Panel window shown in Figure 4-14. To open this window, choose Start⇨Control Panel⇨Ease of Access⇨Speech Recognition.

Figure 4-14

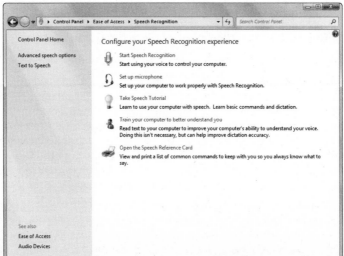

Setting up Speech Recognition

Before you can start barking commands at your Windows 7 computer, you have to get a microphone connected to your PC (preferably with headphones like the ones worn by the telemarketers you know and love). With microphone at the ready, you then have to set up the Speech Recognition feature by following these steps:

1. Click the Start Speech Recognition link in the Speech Recognition Control Panel window (opened by choosing Start⇨Control Panel⇨Ease of Access⇨Speech Recognition).

   Windows 7 displays a Welcome to Speech Recognition dialog box.

2. Click Next and then select the Headset Microphone, Desktop Microphone, or Other option in the Select the Type of Microphone You Would Like to Use dialog box.

3. Click Next and then position the microphone connected to your Windows 7 computer next to your mouth. Click Next in the Set Up Your Microphone dialog box.

4. Read the "Peter dictates to his computer . . . " passage in a normal voice and then, when you finish dictating, click Next.

   If the computer heard you distinctly, the message `The microphone is ready to use with this computer` appears in the Your Microphone Is Now Set Up dialog box. If you see a message indicating that the computer did not hear you very well, click the Back button and repeat Step 4, perhaps after adjusting the microphone's position and making sure that it's properly connected to the computer's microphone jack (and not the speaker jack).

5. Click Next in the Your Microphone Is Now Set Up dialog box.

6. Select the Enable Document Review option in the Improve Speech Recognition Accuracy dialog box and then click Next.

   The Choose an Activation Mode window appears. By default, Windows Speech Recognition selects the manual activation mode whereby speech recognition turns off when you say "stop listening" and then must be manually turned on either by clicking the Microphone button in the Speech Recognition toolbar or by pressing Ctrl+ . If you select the Use Voice Activation Mode option, you can reactivate speech recognition simply by saying "start listening" into your microphone.

7. To turn on Voice Activation mode, click the Use Voice Activation Mode option button before you click Next.

   The Print the Speech Reference Card window appears. This window contains common Speech Recognition commands, including such topics as how to select items on the screen, choose commands, and dictate text.

8. Click the View Reference Sheet button to open a Windows Help and Support window.

9. Click the topics such as Common Speech Recognition Commands, Dictation, and Punctuation Marks and Special Characters to display their information. Click the Print button on the window's toolbar if you want to print any of these expanded help topics.

10. Click the Close button in the Windows Help and Support window.

11. Click the Next button to open the Run Speech Recognition Every Time I Start the Computer dialog box.

    By default, Windows 7 selects the Run Speech Recognition at Startup check box. If you don't want Windows to automatically start the Speech Recognition feature each time you boot Windows 7, deselect this check box before you proceed.

12. Click the Next button to open the You Can Now Control This Computer By Voice dialog box.

13. Click the Start Tutorial button to run the Speech Recognition Tutorial, which is both necessary to train the computer to understand your voice as well as being very good for practice.

After you finish the Speech Recognition Tutorial, Windows 7 automatically returns you to the Speech Recognition Control Panel window. The sleeping Speech Recognition toolbar now appears docked in the center at the top of the Windows desktop (indicated by the word "Off" in the toolbar rather than "Listening").

To undock the Speech Recognition toolbar and move it to a new position on the Windows 7 desktop, drag the toolbar by any area outside the microphone icon, the level meter, Close, and Minimize buttons. To hide the toolbar (while still running the Speech Recognition feature) as an icon in the Notification area of the Windows taskbar, click the Speech toolbar's Minimize button.

Remember, if you selected Voice Activation mode, you can say "Start Listening" in your microphone whenever you want the sleeping Speech Recognition feature to wake up and start listening to what you have to say. Otherwise, if you used the default manual setting, you need to click the Microphone button in the Speech Recognition toolbar before you can start jabbering Windows commands!

Changing Speech Recognition settings

After initially setting up Speech Recognition on your Windows 7 computer, you can modify its settings by using the options on the Speech Recognition tab of the Speech Properties dialog box shown in Figure 4-15. To open this dialog box with this tab selected, click the Advanced Speech Options link in Navigation pane of the Speech Recognition Control Panel window (which in turn is opened by choosing Start⇨Control Panel⇨Ease of Access⇨Speech Recognition).

The options on the Speech Recognition tab of the Speech Properties dialog box are divided into four areas:

- **Language,** where you can select a new language other than the default English in which to dictate commands and text (assuming that you installed other Language Packs for use with Windows 7)

- **Recognition Profiles,** where you can create new speech profiles for different users on the same computer and then select them for use with the Speech Recognition feature

- **User Settings,** where you enable or disable the Run Speech Recognition At Startup and the Allow Computer to Review Your Documents and Mail to Improve Speech Recognition Accuracy features

- **Microphone,** where you can select a new microphone to use in Speech Recognition (by clicking the Audio Input button) and then get it ready for use with Speech Recognition (by clicking the Configure Microphone button)

Figure 4-15

Modifying the Text to Speech Settings

If you use Excel 2003 or later, you can use Windows' Text to Speech capabilities to have your computer read aloud a series of entries that you've made in cell ranges in your worksheet. (Unfortunately, Excel is the only Office application that currently supports this great Text to Speech feature.) Text to Speech comes in very handy when you need to check the correctness of a series of cell entries and want to hear their values read back to you as you visually verify them on a separate printed page.

When you use Text to Speech with Excel (or another program that supports Text to Speech), you can modify two Text to Speech settings:

- ✔ **Voice Selection:** By default, Windows uses a female voice called Microsoft Anna who speaks American English (the only digital voice that Microsoft includes with Windows 7). However, you can add other digital voices and, if you do, replace Anna with any of them to be used in any programs that support Text to Speech.

- ✔ **Voice Speed:** By default, Windows selects Normal as the voice speed but you can make it faster or slower.

To change these settings, you open the Speech Properties dialog box with the Text to Speech tab selected (Start⇨Control Panel⇨Ease of Access⇨Text to Speech). To select a new voice, click it on Voice Selection drop-down menu. To select a new voice speed, drag the slider in the Voice Speed area to the left to make the voice slower or to the right to make it faster. Then, click the Preview Voice button to listen to your changes before you click OK.

If you're using Excel 2003, in order to use Text to Speech to proof cell entries, you simply display the Text to Speech toolbar (View⇨Toolbars⇨Text to Speech). If you're using Excel 2007, however, you first need to add the Speak commands to the Excel Quick Access toolbar before you can use the Windows Text to Speech feature. To do so, launch Excel 2007, click the Customize Quick Access Toolbar button at the end of the Quick Access toolbar and then click More Commands on the menu. Excel then opens the Excel Options dialog box. Select All Commands in the Choose Commands From drop-down menu in this dialog box and then scroll down in the list box below until you see the commands, Speak Cells, Speak Cells – Stop Speaking Cells and so on. Select each of the Speak commands you want to add to the toolbar followed by the Add command and then click OK. For more on using Windows Text to Speech in Excel 2007, see my *Excel 2007 For Dummies* or *Excel 2007 All-in-One Desk Reference For Dummies* (both from Wiley Publishing).

Windows Fax and Scan

The Windows Fax and Scan utility enables you to send or receive and organize faxes via your Windows 7 computer as well as scan documents and pictures, provided that you have a scanner connected to your computer. You can even use the utility's two features together by faxing a document that you've scanned.

To launch the Windows Fax and Scan utility, choose Start⇨All Programs⇨Windows Fax and Scan. Windows 7 then opens a Windows Fax and Scan window, as shown in Figure 4-16.

As you can see in this figure, at the bottom of the Navigation pane of the Windows Fax and Scan window you find two buttons: Faxes and Scans. You click these buttons to switch between the fax and scanning features.

Figure 4-16

To be able to send and receive faxes with Windows Fax and Scan, your computer must either be connected to a fax server that's part of your computer network, or you must have a phone line connected to a fax modem installed on your computer. (You can't use separate fax machines.) To be able to scan documents and pictures, you must have a scanner installed on your computer.

Sending and receiving faxes

Before you can send and receive a fax with the Windows Fax and Scan utility, you must set up a fax account for yourself. To do the setup, choose Tools➪Fax Accounts from the main menu of the Windows Fax and Scan window when the Faxes button is selected. Then click the Add button to open a Create Fax Account dialog box, where you click either the Fax Modem Connection or Windows Fax Server, depending upon whether you use a fax modem or a server to send and receive faxes.

After you set up your fax account, you can use it to create a new fax to send. Simply click the New Fax button on the toolbar in the Windows Fax and Scan window to open the New Fax dialog box, where you can select a cover page, select the contact to whom to delivery the fax, and input the text of the fax message.

Don't forget that you can insert text that you've already typed in another document in the body of the fax via the Windows Clipboard. (Press Ctrl+C to copy the selected text and Ctrl+V to insert it into the New Fax dialog box.) You can also attach a text document to the fax message with the Attach button on the New Fax toolbar, insert a picture in the body of the fax with the Insert Picture button, and insert a scanned document or picture in the body of the fax with the Insert From Scanner button.

When you finish composing the new fax, have Windows 7 send it by clicking the Send button in the New Fax dialog box.

To receive a fax you're expecting in the open Windows Fax and Scan window, click the Receive a Fax Now button on the window's toolbar.

Scanning documents

Before you can scan a document with the Windows Fax and Scan utility, your scanner must be listed in the Devices section of the Devices and Printers Control Panel window (which, if Windows doesn't automatically find it, you can manually add in the Devices and Printers window opened by choosing Start➪ Devices and Printers). To scan a document, open the Windows Fax and Scan window and then click the Scan button in the Navigation pane before you click the New Scan button on the far left of the window's toolbar.

Windows 7 then opens a New Scan dialog box for your scanner, where you can preview the document and then scan the final version. To save the scanned document, click the Save As button and then enter the filename, select the type of graphics file you want the scanned document to be saved as, and then click the Save button.

To automatically forward the document you just scanned as an attachment to a new fax message, click the Forward as Fax button.

The scan feature in the Windows Fax and Scan utility is set primarily to scan text documents. If you want to scan a photograph or other graphic, keep in mind that you can do so directly from within the Windows Live Photo Gallery. (*See* Part 8 for more on Windows Live Photo Gallery.)

System and Security

The foremost utility for system maintenance and security in Windows 7 is the Control Panel, as shown in the following figure. The Control Panel enables you to control computer settings relating to both hardware components and Windows software, along with overall security and individual user accounts. In addition, this part of the book gives you the specifics on backing up the data on your computer and keeping your copy of the Windows 7 operating system up-to-date.

In this part . . .

- ✔ **Backing Up and Restoring Your Computer System**
- ✔ **Changing Your Computer's Security Settings with the Control Panel**
- ✔ **Managing User Accounts on Your Computer**
- ✔ **Getting Automatic Windows Updates**

Backup and Restore

The Backup and Restore utility gives you access to the Windows Backup utility that you can use to make, compare, or restore backup copies of selected files and folders on your computer as well as your entire hard drive (unless you're running the Home Basic or Home Premium version, in which case you don't have this program). Use this utility to maintain copies of all the files you can't live without, in case (knock on wood) anything ever happens to your computer or the hard drive.

To open the Backup and Restore window (similar to the one shown in Figure 5-1), choose Start⇨Control Panel⇨Back Up Your Computer.

Figure 5-1

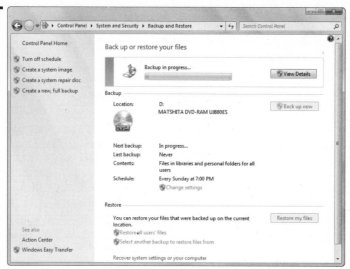

Setting up the backup

The first time you open the Windows Backup utility, you need to set up how you want the backup to take place. Using the Backup and Restore window, you'll want to designate the drive on which you want the backups stored as well as the schedule that you want Windows to follow in backing up the files on your computer's hard drive.

To set up the backup, follow these steps:

1. Click the Set Up Backup button in the Backup and Restore window (Start⇨ Control Panel⇨System and Maintenance⇨Back Up Your Computer).

    Windows opens the Select Where You Want to Save Your Backup screen in the Set Up Backup dialog box, where you specify the drive on which you want the backup files stored.

2. Select the computer drive (other than the hard drive with the files you're going to back up) on which you want to back up your files in the Save Backup On list box. If your computer is connected to a network and you want to save your computer's file on one of the network drives, click the Save on a Network button, specify the drive in the Network Location text box, and then enter your user ID and password in their associated text boxes before you click OK.

If you select the DVD drive on your computer, be aware that Windows can't save a complete image of all its system files on this type of removable media. (In order to back up such a system image, you must specify some sort of external drive that's directly connected to your computer or a file share on the drive of a networked computer.) If you're not planning on backing up a complete image of the hard drive with the Windows system, you can specify a DVD drive and back up your files on writable DVDs.

3. Click the Next button.

Windows displays the What Do You Want to Back Up options in the Set Up Backup dialog box, where you specify what libraries and files you want to back up.

By default, the Windows Backup utility backs up all data files on your computer on a regular schedule.

4. If you want to specify which files to back up on your hard drive, select the Let Me Choose option before you click Next.

Windows opens the Review Your Backup Settings screen in the Set Up Backup dialog box so that you can review the backup drive location and which files are to be backed up, along with the time and day the backup is regularly scheduled.

5. (Optional) To change the schedule that Windows 7 uses for making regular backups of your computer's hard drive, click the Change Schedule link and then specify the new schedule using the How Often, What Day, and What Time options in the How Often Do You Want to Back Up screen in the Set Up Backup dialog box. When you're done, click OK.

Windows closes the How Often Do You Want to Back Up screen and returns you to the Review Your Backup Settings screen in the Set Up Backup dialog box.

6. Click the Save Settings and Start Backup button.

Windows then displays the Backup in Progress indicator at the top of the Backup and Restore window (refer to Figure 5-1), which keeps you informed of the backup progress. The operating system backs up all the selected files, first by creating a shadow copy of the files and then by actually copying them to the designated drive, disc, or network folder. While Windows performs the backup, you can continue to work.

To call a halt to a backup before Windows finishes copying all the files, click the Stop Backup button that appears in the Backup Files dialog box.

Restoring backed up files

After using the Windows Backup utility to back up either certain files or your entire computer, you can then use the same utility to restore the backed-up files if you ever need to due to a hard drive malfunction or reformatting.

To restore files and folders backed up with the Windows Backup utility, follow these steps:

1. Click the Restore My Files button in the Restore section of the Backup and Restore window.

   Windows opens the Browse or Search Your Backup for Files and Folders to Restore screen in the Restore Files dialog box.

2. Click the Browse for Folders button to open the Browse the Backup for Folders and Files dialog box where you can select the Backup of C: folder by clicking its icon in the list box, followed by the Add Folder button.

   If you don't want to restore the entire backup of your hard drive, open the Backup of C: folder by double-clicking its icon and continue to open the drive's subfolders and then select the individual folder you want to restore, followed by the Add Folder button.

   To restore individual files, use the Browse for Files or Search button to locate and add the separate files to be restored.

3. When you finish adding the folder(s) and/or files to be restored to the list box in the Browse or Search Your Backup for Files and Folders to Restore screen of the Restore Files dialog box, click the Next button.

   Windows opens the Where Do You Want to Restore Your Files screen in the Restore Files dialog box.

4. (Optional) To have Windows restore the backup files you've specified to a location different from its original location on the hard drive, select the In the Following Location option and then specify the folder path in its text box. If you do *not* want Windows to restore files to their original subfolders in this path, you also need to deselect the Restore the Files to Their Original Subfolders check box.

5. Click the Restore button in the Where Do You Want to Restore Your Files screen of the Restore Files dialog box.

Windows then displays the Restoring Files screen of the Restore Files dialog box that keeps you informed about the progress of the backed up file restoration. When Windows 7 encounters a conflict whereby an existing file on your hard drive will be replaced by a restored backup file, the Copy File dialog box appears.

Select the Copy and Replace option in this dialog box to have Windows 7 replace the original file with its backup equivalent. Select the Don't Copy option to have Windows leave the original file in place, or select the Copy, But Keep Both Files option to have Windows leave the original file while at the same time adding the backup version as an additional file.

 If you want, you can tell Windows 7 to follow the option you select in the Copy File dialog for all subsequent duplicate conflicts during the restoration: Simply select the Do This for All Conflicts check box at the bottom of the Copy File dialog box before you select any of the options.

Control Panel

The Control Panel in Windows 7 is the place to go when you need to make changes to various settings of your computer system. To open the Control Panel, click the Start button on the taskbar and then click Control Panel on the Start menu.

Windows 7 gives you three different views for looking at your computer's Control Panel:

- **Category view** (the default) contains links representing groups of related Control Panel programs displayed in two columns. (See Figure 5-2.)

- **Large Icons view** displays as many of the large, individual Control Panel program icons as can appear in the Control Panel. (See Figure 5-3.)

- **Small Icons view** displays all the small, individual Control Panel program icons in the Control Panel.

To switch from Category view to Large Icons or Small Icons view, click the View By drop-down button (labeled Category) in the upper-right corner of the Control Panel and then choose Large Icons or Small Icons from the button's drop-down menu. Then, to switch back into Category view, click the Category item that appears at the top of the drop-down menu now associated either with the Large Icons or Small Icons button (depending upon which item you previously selected).

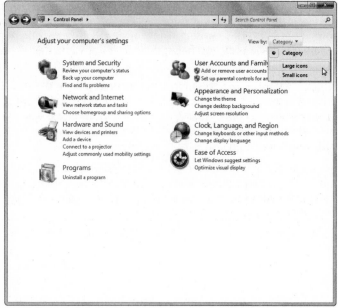

Figure 5-2

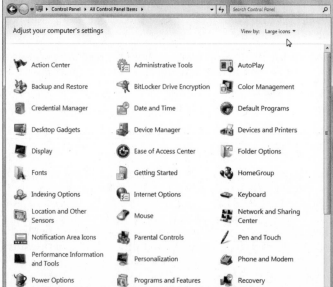

Figure 5-3

As you see in Figure 5-2, in Category view, Windows organizes the Control Panel into eight categories, ranging from System and Security to Ease of Access. To open a window with the Control Panel options for any one of these categories, simply click the category's hyperlink.

In Figure 5-3, you notice that when the Control Panel is in Large Icons view, Windows displays an alphabetical listing (across the rows and down the columns) of all the Control Panel options on your system, from Action Center to Windows Update (not visible in this figure). To view (and possibly change) the settings for a particular Control Panel option in Large Icons or Small Icons, you need to double-click the Control Panel program icon.

The following table gives you a descriptive list of all the Control Panel categories. Use this table to figure out what type of computer settings you can change by clicking each category's hyperlink.

Click This Category Link . . .	*. . . To Display These Groups of Links*
System and Security	Action Center, Windows Firewall, System, Windows Update, Power Options, Backup and Restore, BitLocker Drive Encryption, and Administrative Tools
User Accounts and Family Safety	User Accounts, Parental Controls, Windows Cardspace, Credential Manager, and Mail (32-bit)
Network and Internet	Network and Sharing Center, Homegroup, and Internet Options
Appearance and Personalization	Personalization, Display, Desktop Gadgets, Taskbar and Start Menu, Ease of Access Center, Folder Options, and Fonts
Hardware and Sound	Devices and Printers, AutoPlay, Sound, Power Options, Display, and Windows Mobility Center
Clock, Language, and Region	Date and Time, and Region and Language
Programs	Programs and Features, Default Programs, and Desktop Gadgets
Ease of Access	Ease of Access Center and Speech Recognition

As you can see from this table, the Control Panel programs are numerous, and different categories have duplicate links for opening the same Control Panel windows or dialog boxes. The following sections give you detailed information on the most commonly used Control Panel groups: System and Security; Hardware and Sound; Clock, Language, and Region; and Ease of Access.

See Part 1 for information on customizing your computer with the Personalization and Desktop Gadgets Control Panel programs.

See Part 2 for information on using the Programs and Features and Default Programs Control Panel programs.

See Part 3 for information on configuring and changing network settings with the Network and Internet Control Panel options.

See Part 4 for information on configuring and using speech recognition and text-to-speech with the Speech Recognition Control Panel options.

System and Security

When you click the System and Security link in the Control Panel (when the Category view is selected), Windows opens a new window (see Figure 5-4) containing the following groups of options:

- ✔ **Action Center:** Opens a window displaying your computer's current security status. From this window, you can troubleshoot and resolve any system maintenance and security issues, including modifying the User Account Control settings and updates that need to be installed and backups that need to be made. (***See*** "Backup and Restore" for details earlier in this part.)

- ✔ **Windows Firewall:** Opens a window where you can review the current status of your firewall as well as set up firewall protection for whatever kind of network your computer is connected to.

- ✔ **System:** Opens a window displaying information about your computer system, such as rating (based on its processor, memory, hard drive, and graphics capability), memory, type of operating system (32-bit or 64-bit), and the edition of the Windows operating system (including the product key).

- ✔ **Windows Update:** Opens the Windows Update window, where you can check for updates to the Windows 7 operating system. (***See*** "Windows Update" for details, later in this part.)

- ✔ **Power Options:** Opens the Power Options window, where you can select or edit a power scheme that determines when and whether Windows should turn off your monitor or power down your hard drive after a specified period of inactivity. You can also use the Require Password on Wakeup link in the Navigation pane to designate whether to shut down the computer or put it to sleep when you click the Power button on your computer, and whether to require you to enter your password when you wake your computer from sleep. (***See*** "Restart, Sleep/Hibernate, Lock, Log Off, and Shut Down" in Part 2.)

✔ **Backup and Restore:** Launches the Windows Backup utility, which allows you to back up all or just certain files on your computer's hard drive as well as restore them. (*See* "Backup and Restore" for details, earlier in this part.)

✔ **BitLocker Drive Encryption:** Opens a window where you can protect your hard drive (or any removable data drives you connect to your computer) by encrypting all its files and thus protecting them from unauthorized access and use. When you encrypt a drive, all files that you store on that drive are automatically encrypted, including any shared files. (Don't turn on this drive encryption unless you've thoroughly reviewed the Windows Help and Support article opened by clicking the What Should I Know About BitLocker Drive Encryption Before I Turn It On link that appears in this window. You need to understand how drive encryption works before you use it.)

✔ **Administrative Tools:** Opens the Administrative Tools window, which contains shortcuts to a number of utilities used by the Systems Administrator to review and control your computer. (A word to the wise: Don't fool with these options unless you know what you're doing.)

Figure 5-4

User Accounts

The User Accounts window (see Figure 5-5) appears when you click the User Accounts and Family Safety link in the Control Panel in Category view. This window contains the following options:

✔ **User Accounts:** Opens a second User Accounts window, where you can make changes to your own user account on the computer. You also use this window to modify the User Account Control settings used both to manage accounts for other users that use the same computer and to determine when you would like to be notified of attempts to make changes to the Windows settings — assuming that you're part of the Administrators group that has the permissions to make these changes. (*See* "Modifying User Account settings" later in this part for details.)

✔ **Parental Controls:** Opens the Parental Controls window, where you can manage how children in the household access computers.

✔ **Windows CardSpace:** Opens the Windows CardSpace dialog box, where you can add new information cards that you can then use to securely manage the personal identity information you routinely send to trusted Web sites on the Internet. (*See* "Using Windows CardSpace" later in this part for details.)

✔ **Credential Manager:** Opens the Credential Manager window, where you can securely store the various usernames and passwords that you need to supply in order to access various Web sites. (*See* "Using Credential Manager" later in this part for details.)

✔ **Mail (32-bit):** Opens the Mail Setup dialog box for the e-mail program you use (such as Microsoft Outlook), where you can manage your e-mail accounts as well as modify the file settings for your e-mail program and the e-mail profile that your computer uses.

Figure 5-5

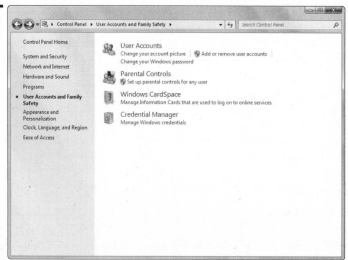

Modifying User Account settings

When you click the User Accounts link in the User Accounts window shown in Figure 5-5, Windows 7 opens a second User Accounts window, similar to the one shown in Figure 5-6. This window can contain these options:

- ✔ **Change Your Password,** which enables you to create a new password (assuming you have one).

- ✔ **Remove Your Password,** which enables you to delete your password.

- ✔ **Change Your Picture,** which lets you select a new picture for your Windows user account that appears at the top of the Windows 7 Start menu. To select a new picture, click it in the gallery that appears when you select this link or click the Browse for Pictures link and select your own photo from one of your Pictures libraries.

 ✔ **Manage Another Account,** which lets you change your account type and add other users to the computer. Note that you can change your account type from Administrator to Standard User, which restricts your ability to make changes to computer settings that affect its security. For you to be able to make the change to Standard User, at least one other user account needs to be currently designated as an administrator.

 ✔ **Change User Account Control Settings,** which lets you change if/when you're to be notified of changes made to your computer. When you click this link to open the User Account Control Settings dialog box, you can use its slider to choose from the following four options:

- *Always Notify Me When* programs try to install software or make changes to my computer and when I make changes to the Windows settings.

- *Default - Notify Me Only When Programs Try to Make Changes to My Computer:* In other words, don't notify me when *I* make changes to Windows settings, only when programs are about to make changes to the computer.

- *Notify Me Only When Programs Try to Make Changes to My Computer (Do Not Dim My Desktop):* The same as the default setting above except that with this one, Windows does not do the dramatic "dim the desktop" thing used to notify you that programs are trying to make changes to the computer.

- *Never Notify Me When* programs try to install software or make changes to my computer and I make changes to the Windows settings.

 If you want to add a password (something I highly recommend for any laptop computer you travel with) or change the current password you use at startup to access the Windows 7 computer, you don't do it from the User Accounts window. Instead, you need to press Ctrl+Alt+Delete from anywhere in Windows to open its blue Shut Down and Switch User screen and from there click the Change a Password option.

Figure 5-6

Using Windows CardSpace

Windows CardSpace is a new utility for managing the personal information that you share with trusted Web sites on the Internet. It enables you to store information cards containing the identity and contact information that social networking Web sites generally require of members when logging on to their forums. The utility also enables you to install information cards supplied by the trusted Web sites that you deal with (also called *managed cards*) that contain all the credit card and other personal identity information that you supply them in the course of doing business with them.

When you click the Windows CardSpace link in the initial User Accounts Control Panel (refer to Figure 5-5), Windows dims the desktop and displays a Windows CardSpace dialog box that shows all the personal information cards you've created along with all the managed information cards you've installed.

To create a new personal information card or install a managed card sent to you from a trusted Web site, click the Add a Card icon. Windows 7 then opens an Add a Card dialog box containing the following two options:

- ✔ **Create a Personal Card** containing encrypted personal identity information that you can send to trusted Web sites upon their request in order to make it easier to register with them and log on to them.

- ✔ **Install a Managed Card** to add an encrypted information card sent to you by a trusted Web site that contains the personal and credit information you supplied to the site in order to business with it.

After adding personal and managed cards to your Windows CardSpace, you can review their information by clicking their icons in the Your Cards list box and then clicking the Preview button. To edit information in particular fields of the card, click the Edit button.

Using Credential Manager

The Credential Manager window (shown in Figure 5-7) enables you to securely store log on information (user ID and passwords) that you routinely supply to trusted Web sites in order to obtain access to their services. This Control Panel window handles three distinct types of information:

- ✔ **Windows Credentials** that store the network addresses, usernames, and passwords required for you to access various company intranet and SharePoint sites.

- ✔ **Certificate-Based Credentials** that store digitally signed public key certificates that identify you and your computer. These encrypted certificates contain not only your user ID information but your passwords as well and can therefore be used to log you in to highly secure Web sites.

- ✔ **General Credentials** that store the URL addresses, usernames, and passwords required for you to access the other (usually commercial) Web sites you deal with that require you to log on in order to conduct business with them.

To add a new credential to any of these three types, click the Add A link that appears to the right of its name to open a Control Panel window where you can specify all the username, password, network, Internet, certificate information that the particular type of credential requires.

Use the Back Up Vault link in the Credential Manager window to back up all the credentials you add (preferably, on a removable hard or flash drive that you store in a very secure place). That way, you can recover all your user IDs and passwords with the Restore Vault link in the event that your hard drive becomes damaged and its data unusable.

Hardware and Sound

When you click the Hardware and Sound link in the Control Panel when it's in Category view, Windows opens a new Hardware and Sound window (similar to the one shown in Figure 5-8). The Hardware and Sound window displays a list of links that give you access to various hardware devices connected to your computer as well as the ability to modify different hardware-related computer settings. These include hardware devices such as scanners, printers, and webcams as well as sound, power, and display options. It also gives you access to the Windows Mobility Center, an all-in-one panel where you can quickly modify your computer's display brightness, volume, and power-saving scheme as well as its wireless networking, secondary display monitor, synchronization, and presentation settings.

Figure 5-7

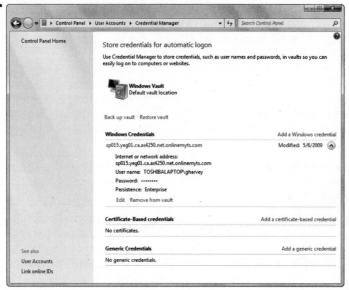

The Hardware and Sound options include the following:

- **Devices and Printers** enables you to change the settings for the various devices (including webcams and your computer's mouse) as well as the printers you've installed on your computer. You can also add a new local or network printer. (*See* "Devices and Printers" later in this part for details.)

- **AutoPlay** enables you to designate which Windows program to use in playing various types of media files. (*See* "AutoPlay" later in this part for details.)

- **Sound** enables you to manage your sound devices and assign new sounds to common Windows events. (*See* "Sound" later in this part for details.)

- **Power Options** enables you to select a new power plan for your computer as well as define the function of the computer's Power button and the function of closing the lid on a laptop computer (by default, it puts the laptop into Sleep mode).

- **Display** enables you to change the relative size of the text on your computer screen as well as adjust various settings such as the pixel resolution and brightness.

- **Windows Mobility Center** opens a Windows Mobility Center dialog box that enables you to adjust a variety of different settings when using a laptop computer running Windows 7 to display a presentation (usually a slide presentation created with PowerPoint) to a live audience on an external projector or monitor.

Figure 5-8

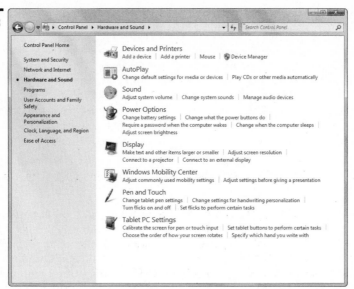

✔ **Pen and Touch** opens a Pen and Touch dialog box (assuming you have a digital tablet) that enables you to modify sensitivity settings and assign functions to its buttons.

✔ **Tablet PC Settings** opens a Tablet PC dialog box where you can calibrate the screen sensitivity (assuming you have a Tablet PC).

Devices and Printers

When you click the View Devices and Printers link under Hardware and Sound in the Control Panel (refer to Figure 5-2) or the Devices and Printer link on the Hardware and Sound window, Windows opens a Devices and Printers window that displays all the external devices (such as a webcam or a mouse) connected to your computer above all printers — physical, virtual (one that simulates a certain type of physical printer such as PDF printer by adding printer-specific codes to a new file rather than producing a printed copy), local, and network — that you've installed.

Adding and managing printers

To add a new local printer to your computer system in the Devices and Printers window, follow these steps:

 1. Click the Add a Printer button on the Devices and Printers window toolbar to start the Add Printer Wizard, make sure that the Add Local Printer option is selected, and then click Next.

2. Select the port for the printer to use in the Use an Existing Port drop-down list in the Select a Printer Port dialog box and then click Next.

3. Click the manufacturer and the model of the printer in the Manufacturers and Printers list boxes, respectively, of the Install Printer Driver dialog box. If you have a disk with the software for the printer, put it into your CD-ROM/DVD drive and then click the Have Disk button: Select the drive that contains this disk in the Copy Manufacturer's Files From drop-down list and then click OK. If you don't have the disk, click the Windows Update button.

4. Click the Next button to advance to the Type a Printer Name dialog box. If you want, edit the name for the printer in the Printer Name text box before you click Next.

5. If you want to share the printer you're installing with other computers connected to your network, you may edit the printer name that appears in the Share Name text box as well as add a description of its location and comments about the shared printer in the Location and Comment text boxes, respectively. If you don't want to share the printer with other computers on the network, select the Do Not Share This Printer option (which automatically deselects the default Share This Printer So That Others on Your Network Can Find and Use It option) before you click Next.

6. To print a test page from your newly installed printer, click the Print a Test Page button in the Add a Printer dialog box before you click the Finish button to finish installing the new printer.

To use the Add Printer Wizard to install a printer that's available through your local area network, follow these (slightly different) steps:

1. Click the Add a Printer button on the Devices and Printers window toolbar and then select the Add a Network, Wireless, or Bluetooth Printer option before you click Next.

2. After Windows is finished searching for all printers on your network as well as all wireless printers in your vicinity, click the name of the printer to install in the Searching for Network Printers list box; then click Next.

3. (Optional) If the printer you want to install is not on this list or Windows fails to find and list the network or wireless printer, click the The Printer I Am Looking For Wasn't Listed link. To browse for the printer on the network, select the Browse for a Printer option and then click Next. To enter the pathname for the printer, leave the Select a Shared Printer by Name option selected and then type the pathname in its text box or use the Browse button to locate it before you click Next.

If you can't locate the printer on the network by browsing and don't know its pathname but do happen to know its IP (Internet Protocol) address, select the Add a Printer Using TCP/IP Address or Hostname option before you click Next. Then enter the IP address in the Host Name or IP Address text box, its port in the Port Name text box, and click Next. Windows then detects the printer, using the address you provide. After Windows locates the printer, click Next.

4. In the Ready to Install Printer dialog box, edit the name for the printer in the Printer Name text box if you want before you click Next.

5. To print a test page from the newly installed printer, click the Print a Test Page button in the Add a Printer dialog box before you click the Finish button to finish installing the new printer.

In addition to installing new printers in the Devices and Printers window, you can use its printer icons in the Printers and Faxes section to change printer settings and to control the jobs you send to it:

✔ **To change the default printer** for your computer programs, right-click the printer's icon and then choose Set as Default Printer from the shortcut menu that appears.

✔ **To share a printer,** assuming that the administrator of the computer has configured the Windows firewall to permit printer sharing, right-click its printer icon and then choose Printer Properties from its shortcut menu. Click the Sharing tab in the Properties dialog box, select the Share This Printer check box, and then give the printer a share name in the Share Name text box provided. To change the layout, paper, and print quality settings for a particular printer, you modify the appropriate settings on the General or Advanced tab of this Properties dialog box.

✔ **To open the currently selected printer when it's processing or printing a print job** (either to view the status of the jobs in the print queue or to cancel print jobs), right-click the printer's icon and then choose See What's Printing from its shortcut menu to open a dialog box for that printer. To pause a print job that's in progress, choose Document⇨Pause from the pull-down menu. To cancel a job, click the print job listed in the queue and then choose Document⇨Cancel.

 To be able to print documents directly from Windows 7, rather than from within a particular program, create a desktop shortcut to your printer by right-clicking its icon in the Printers window and then selecting Create Shortcut from its shortcut menu. Then, simply drag the icon of the file you want printed and drop it on the printer's desktop shortcut. Windows 7 responds by opening that file in the program associated with its file type. That program then immediately sends the file to that printer for printing.

Adding and managing other devices

The Devices and Printers window shows you not only the printer's you've installed on your computer but also all the other devices connected to it — both physically (by some sort of USB or other type of cable) and virtually (by a wireless, infrared, or Bluetooth connection).

Windows 7 automatically attempts to install all new devices that you connect to your computer, and, in most cases, it does a pretty good job of locating the driver necessary to successfully install it. After Windows 7 installs a newly connected device, its icon then appears in the Devices section at the top of the Devices and Printers window.

To get information about a particular device such as a mouse, webcam, scanner, or camera that's connected to your computer and possibly adjust its settings, right-click its icon in the Devices section of the Devices and Printers window and then choose Properties from its shortcut menu. Note that these device icons actually include one for the computer itself, and you can use its shortcut menu to change all manner of computer settings as well as view its properties.

If you don't see your device listed in this Devices section of the Devices and Printers window, click the Add Device button on the Devices and Printers toolbar and then use the device's Installation Wizard to manually install the device.

To scan a text document with a scanner shown in the Devices section of the Devices and Printers window, you need to use the Windows Fax and Scan utility — *see* "Windows Fax and Scan" in Part 4.

AutoPlay

When you click the AutoPlay link in the Hardware and Sound window, Windows opens a separate AutoPlay window. This window displays the various types of audio, video, and image files you can have on your computer in the Media column on the left. You can then specify that a particular program (such as the Windows Media Player or Media Center) open certain kinds of media files, or have Windows take a particular action with certain types of media. For example, you can have Windows 7 open them from Windows Explorer or burn them to disc by selecting Windows Media Player from the drop-down list to the immediate right of that kind of media file.

See "Media Center" and "Windows Media Player" in Part 6 for details on using these Windows programs to play your media files.

Sound

When you click the Sound link in the Hardware and Sound window, Windows opens the Sound dialog box, which contains the following four tabs:

- ✔ **Playback:** Lists all the audio output devices connected to your computer. To review the properties for a particular device or modify its parameters, click the device to select it and then click the Properties button to open a Properties dialog box for that device showing all the options you can change.

- ✔ **Recording:** Enables you to select a new recording device, such as an external microphone or line in.

✔ **Sounds:** Lets you modify or create a new sound scheme that determines what sounds, if any, to play when particular events take place, such as closing programs, displaying an alert box, receiving new e-mail, emptying the Recycle Bin, and so on.

✔ **Communications:** Lets you specify how Windows 7 adjusts the volume of other sounds when it detects you're using the computer to place or receive telephone calls. Your choices are to have Windows automatically Mute All Other Sounds, Reduce the Volume of Other Sounds by 80% (the default setting), Reduce the Volume of Other Sounds by 50%, or Do Nothing.

TIP

To manage the overall volume setting for your computer as well as for the applications on your system that play sound, either click the Adjust System Volume link under Sound in the Hardware and Sound window or right-click the speaker icon in the notification area of the taskbar and then choose Open Volume Mixer from the shortcut menu that appears. Windows then opens a Volume Mixer dialog box, which contains both a Device (for the speakers currently selected) and an Applications slider that you can drag up to increase the volume or down to decrease it. Note that you can move the Applications volume slider independently of the Device slider.

Clock, Language, and Region

When you click the Clock, Language, and Region link in the Control Panel, Windows opens a new Clock, Language, and Region window containing the two following links:

✔ **Date and Time,** which lets you open the Date and Time Properties dialog box, where you can reset the date and time and add up to two additional clocks. (*See* the "Date and Time" section that follows.)

✔ **Region and Language,** which lets you open the Region and Language dialog box, where you can change the way numbers, currency, dates, and times are normally displayed in Windows 7, change the locality of your computer, and add new languages and keyboards to use. (*See* "Region and Language" later in this part.)

Date and Time

When you click the Date and Time link in the Clock, Language, and Region window, Windows opens the Date and Time Properties dialog box with the Date and Time tab selected, as shown in Figure 5-9. You can use the options on this tab to correct the date or time used by your computer as well as to update your time zone and observance of Daylight Saving Time. Note that Windows uses the date and time information displayed on the tab of this dialog box not only to date-stamp files that you create and modify, but also for its time display at the far right of the notification area of the Windows taskbar.

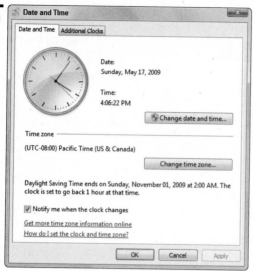

Figure 5-9

You can use the options on the Additional Clocks tab to keep tabs on the local times in other time zones besides your own. Just select the Additional Clock 1 or Additional Clock 2 check box and then select the time zone in the associated drop-down list for the new clock. Give it a name in its Enter Display Name text box before you click OK.

After adding more clocks, you can check their local time anytime you want simply by clicking the local time that appears at the far right of the notification area of the Windows 7 taskbar. Doing so displays a Date and Time Settings pop-up bar that contains a monthly calendar with the current date in red along with analog representations of all your clocks on your computer with their current times. (Simply click anywhere on the desktop outside this Date and Time Settings bar to hide its display.)

Figure 5-10 shows the Date and Time Settings bar that appears when I click the local time displayed on my taskbar. This display contains a calendar with the current month, lists the current time, and shows all the clocks I've created. In this figure, you can see that I've created two additional clocks: an Indianapolis clock (that uses the Indiana East setting that makes this time the same as New York City), so I always know my publisher's local time, and a Hawaii clock, so that I know the local time of the place where I'll be when I get the book done! To get rid of this date and time display, simply click anywhere on the desktop outside of its graphic.

TIP

To have Windows open a temporary pop-up display that lists the current date and the time for the system clock and each of the clocks you've created, simply position the mouse pointer on the time in the notification area. This pop-up display then disappears the moment you move the mouse pointer off the time in the notification area.

Figure 5-10

Region and Language

When you click the Region and Language link in the Clock, Language, and Region window, Windows opens the Region and Language dialog box with the Formats tab selected, as shown in Figure 5-11. Here, you can select a new date and time format for the computer in one fell swoop — going to the standard European day/month/year instead of the United States–style month/day/year, for example — by clicking the Format drop-down button and selecting the language and country from its drop-down list, such as French (Canada) or French (France).

To further customize and tweak the default number, currency, and date formats on your computer, click the Additional Settings button on the Formats tab to open the Customize Format dialog box, where you then click the appropriate tab (Numbers, Currency, Time, or Date) and use the individual drop-down lists to modify all the settings of the selected format that you need to change.

To select a new country location for your computer, click the Location tab in the Region and Language dialog box and then select the new country from the Current Location drop-down list.

To switch to a new keyboard or language or to make changes to the language bar settings, click the Keyboards and Languages tab in the Region and Language dialog box and then click the Change Keyboards button to open the Text Services and Input Languages dialog box. There, you can use the options on the General tab to add and select new input languages for Windows as well as a new keyboard layout for those languages.

Figure 5-11

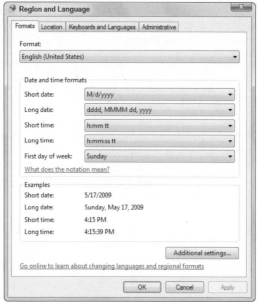

To control how the Language bar (which enables you to switch from using one language to another while working in Windows programs) appears on the desktop, click the Language Bar tab in the Text Services and Input Languages dialog box. Use its options and check boxes to modify its desktop behavior.

To change the hot keys you can use to switch from one language to another in Windows (instead of having to do this from the Language bar), click the Advanced Key Settings tab in the Text Services and Input Languages dialog box and then click the language for which you want to select a set of predefined hot keys. Click the Change Key Sequence button to open the Change Key Sequence dialog box. There, select the option for the predefined sequence under Switch Input Language before you click OK.

To add or remove languages on your computer, click the Install/Uninstall Languages button on the Keyboard and Languages tab of the Region and Language dialog box. Windows opens the Install or Uninstall Display Languages dialog box, where you select either the Install Display Languages option to add new languages to the computer (provided that you have already copied their language files on your computer and know their location) or the Uninstall Display Languages option to delete them.

Ease of Access

When you click the Ease of Access link in the Control Panel, Windows opens an Ease of Access window, which contains the following two links:

✔ **Ease of Access Center,** which leads to an Ease of Access Center window, which contains a whole range of options for aiding users with various degrees of vision and hearing impairments.

✔ **Speech Recognition,** which leads to a Configure Your Speech Recognition Experience window, where you can set up speech recognition on your computer so that you can issue voice commands as well as dictate text in Windows application programs. (*See* "Speech Recognition" in Part 4 for details).

When you click the Ease of Access Center link, the Ease of Access Center Control Panel window, shown in Figure 5-12, appears. The controls in this window enable you to change a number of keyboard, sound, display, and mouse settings that can make using the computer easier if you have less-than-perfect physical dexterity. The Quick Access to Common Tools section of this window contains the following check box options in two columns:

✔ **Start Magnifier:** Turns on and off the Microsoft Screen Magnify window that shows each element of the screen magnified many times. Use the settings in the Microsoft Screen Magnify dialog box that appears when you first turn on this feature to control various settings, including whether the Screen Magnify window appears full screen at startup and assigning a new magnification factor (which is 2x by default).

✔ **Start On-Screen Keyboard:** Turns on and off the display of the On-Screen Keyboard. The On-Screen Keyboard enables you to make text entries by clicking its keys to input letters, numbers, and punctuation, plus the accelerator keys (Shift, Ctrl, and Alt), function keys (F1 through F12), and cursor keys (Tab, Home, End, ←, ↑, →, ↓, and so on). Don't confuse this On-Screen Keyboard window with the Input PC Panel. The Input PC Panel enables you to make keyboard entries via written inputs with the mouse or a special pen tablet connected to your PC or directly on the screen of a Tablet PC running Windows 7.

✔ **Start Narrator:** Turns on and off the Narrator feature, which reads aloud the names of each key you press, all system messages and onscreen messages that you receive, as well as all menu and toolbar options you select with the mouse.

✔ **Set Up High Contrast:** Turns on and off High Contrast, which displays all Windows elements in very high contrasting colors. Click the Setup High Contrast to open a Personalization dialog box, where you can select the high contrast color scheme to use.

 Windows automatically uses the Text to Speech feature to narrate the name of each check box option while highlighting it whenever the Ease of Access Center window is open, provided that you don't deselect the Always Read This Section Aloud and the Always Scan This Section check boxes at the bottom of the Quick Access to Common Tools section.

In addition to these options in the Quick Access to Common Tools section, this window contains the following links in the Explore All Settings section, which you can fine-tune to make your PC easier to use:

✔ **Use the Computer without a Display:** Opens a window of audio accessibility options — including Narrator and Audio Description — that make it possible for a user with a major visual impairment to interact with the computer through audio cues.

✔ **Make the Computer Easier to See:** Opens a window of visual accessibility options, such as turning on the Magnifier and increasing the thickness of the blinking cursor that make it easier for a user with some degree of visual impairment to see and decipher screen elements.

✔ **Use the Computer without a Mouse or Keyboard:** Opens a window containing options for activating the On-Screen Keyboard and enabling you to configure and activate Speech Recognition (*see* Part 4) on your computer.

Figure 5-12

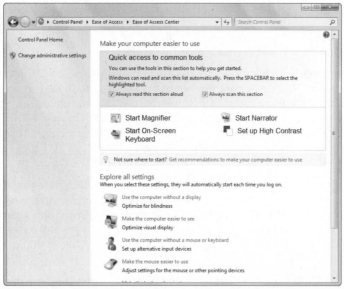

✔ **Make the Mouse Easier to Use:** Opens a window with mouse settings you can adjust, including activating Mouse Keys, which enables you to use the numeric keypad to move the mouse.

✔ **Make the Keyboard Easier to Use:** Opens a window with keyboard options that you can adjust, including Mouse Keys (see above), Sticky Keys, Toggle Keys (to sound a tone when you press the Caps Lock, Num Lock, or Scroll Lock keys), and Filter Keys.

✔ **Use Text or Visual Alternatives for Sounds:** Opens a window of text and visual alternatives for sound options, including turning on Sound Sentry to display visual onscreen warnings (rather than audible ones) and text captions for spoken dialog when that's available.

✔ **Make It Easier to Focus on Tasks:** Opens a window containing options for configuring and turning on the Narrator as well as Sticky Keys (a feature that enables you to press keyboard shortcuts such as Ctrl+Alt+Delete one key at a time), Toggle Keys (to hear a tone when you press keys like CAPS, LOCK, and NUM LOCK), and Filter Keys (to ignore or slow down repeated keystrokes as well as adjust keyboard repeat rates), and to control Windows onscreen animations.

Windows Update

The Windows Update feature notifies you of the latest updates and bug fixes for the Windows 7 operating system directly from the Microsoft Web site. You can set Windows Update to automatically download Windows updates on a regular schedule and have it either ask you to install them on your computer or install them automatically.

To launch Windows Update, choose Start⇨Control Panel⇨System and Security⇨Windows Update. Windows then opens a Windows Update window similar to the one shown in Figure 5-13. This window informs you of any updates that are available for downloading but not yet installed on your computer and enables you to download and install them by clicking the Install Updates button (which appears when important updates are available). It also enables you to select optional updates for downloading and installing (by clicking Optional Updates link, selecting them, and then clicking the Install Updates button that appears) as well as to review all updates that have already been made to your system using the Windows Update feature (by clicking the View Update History link in the Navigation pane).

You can also open the Windows Update window from the Start menu by choosing Start⇨All Programs⇨Windows Update.

To turn automatic updates off and on, as well as to modify how often Windows checks for and downloads and/or installs updates, follow these steps:

1. Open the Windows Update window (Start⇨Control Panel⇨System and Security⇨Windows Update) and then click the Change Settings link in its Navigation pane.

Windows opens a Change Settings window similar to the one shown in Figure 5-14, where Windows automatically selects the Install Updates Automatically (Recommended) option on the Important Updates button.

Figure 5-13

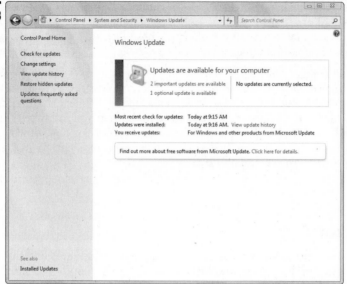

2. (Optional) To change how often and at what time Windows installs new updates to your computer, click the Install New Updates drop-down list button and select the day of the week (Every Sunday through Every Saturday). Next click the time drop-down list button to the right and select the time of day (12:00 AM midnight to 11:00 PM).

3. To prevent Windows from automatically downloading and installing updates on your computer, select the appropriate option for the type of updating you want to put into effect:

   • *Download Updates but Let Me Choose Whether to Install Them:* With this option, Windows automatically checks for and downloads critical and security updates, but you can then review them in the Windows Update window and install them if you choose by clicking the Install Updates button.

   • *Check for Updates but Let Me Choose Whether to Download and Install Them:* With this option, Windows only checks for updates. You need to then open the Windows Update window and click the Download and Install button to actually install them.

   • *Never Check for Updates (Not Recommended):* Selecting this option turns off the Windows Update feature entirely.

4. (Optional) Modify any of the additional update settings in this window that you want to change: Give Me Recommended Updates the Same Way I Receive Important Updates (selected under Recommended Updates), Allow All Users to Install Updates (selected under Who Can Install Updates), Give Me Updates for Microsoft Products and Check for New Optional Microsoft Software When I Update Windows (selected under Microsoft Update), and Show Me Detailed Notifications When New Microsoft Software Is Available (not selected under Software Notification).

Keep in mind that when you deselect the Give Me Recommended Updates the Same Way I Receive Important Updates check box, Windows Update no longer checks optional updates to your system (such as the latest drivers for hardware on your system) that can greatly improve the performance of your system.

5. Click OK or press Enter to close the Change Settings window.

Figure 5-14

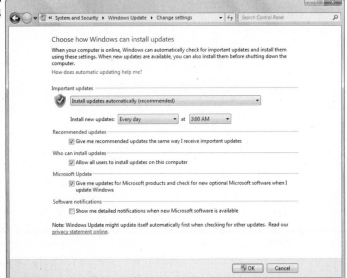

Click the View Update History link in the Windows Update window to open the View Update History window, which displays a complete log of all updates made to your computer with Windows Update. This update log includes the name of the update, its current status, type (Recommended or Important), as well as the date of installation.

Entertainment

Windows 7 is full of fun stuff to keep you entertained. The diversions run the gamut from games to making your computer a part of your larger home entertainment center, thanks to Windows Media Center, shown in the following figure. Also part of the fun is the DVD Maker that you can use to save your digital movies and slide shows on DVDs and the Windows Media Player that you can use to play music, create playlists, rip tracks from audio CDs, and burn CDs.

In this part . . .

- Playing Games on Your PC
- Listening to Music, Viewing Photos, and Watching TV with the Media Center
- Creating and Burning DVDs with Windows DVD Maker
- Playing Music and DVDs with Windows Media Player

Games

Let the games begin! To open the Games window, similar to the one shown in Figure 6-1, all you have to do is choose Start⇨Games. To play any of the games included with Windows, double-click the game icon or right-click the icon and then choose Play from its shortcut menu. Windows then opens the game in its own window.

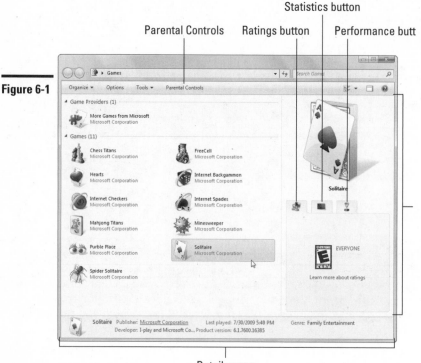

Figure 6-1

Statistics button

Parental Controls   Ratings button   Performance butt

Details pane

If you have the Classic menus displayed in the Games window, you can also launch the game selected in the window by choosing File⇨Play.

When you select a game in the Games window, the Details pane along the bottom of the Games window displays not only general information about the game's publisher and developer, but also the date you last played the game. In addition, the Preview pane on the right side of the Games window displays the game's rating. By the way, you don't have to worry about the content: All games supplied with Windows are rated E for Everyone.

If you want to check the performance of the game on your computer (given its current performance rating running Windows 7), click the Performance button that appears to the right of the Ratings button under the game icon in the Preview pane. When you select the Solitaire game, Windows adds a Statistics button to the immediate left of the Performance button (see Figure 6-1). When you click this button, the Solitaire Preview pane displays a whole bunch of game stats, including your high score, the total number of games you've won and lost, your win percentage, and your longest winning and losing streaks.

Remember that you can get help on the rules for playing the game you've launched by choosing Help⇨View Help from the game window's menu or by pressing F1.

If you have to close a game before you've had a chance to win, Windows gives you the option of saving the game in its present state when you close the game's window. If you want Windows to save your game when you exit it, click the Save button in Exit Game dialog box. The next time you open the program for the game that you've saved, Windows opens a Saved Game Found alert dialog box that asks whether you want to continue your saved game. To open the saved game rather than start a new one, click the Yes button in this alert dialog box.

Media Center

Windows 7 integrates the Media Center as a part of its entertainment programs. Originally developed as an interface for what was once dubbed the Media Center PC (a computer running Windows XP that's specially configured for playing multimedia and often is equipped with a TV tuner card and a special wireless remote), you can use the Windows version of this nifty application to play music, view your digital pictures, play movies, and even watch and record TV (assuming that your computer is equipped with a TV tuner card).

Keep in mind that you can connect your computer that runs the Media Center for Windows directly to your home entertainment center by purchasing the Media Center Extender. You can connect your computer directly to your Xbox 360 by purchasing the Media Center Extender for Xbox.

The first time you launch the Media Center, you see the Welcome to the Media Center Wizard, which walks you through the steps of setting up the center for your screen display, configuring it to receive a TV signal and downloading the online TV guide — if your computer is equipped with a TV tuner card.

Thereafter, whenever you launch the Media Center (Start⇨All Programs⇨ Windows Media Center), the program opens full screen in a predominantly dark-blue window, similar to the one shown in Figure 6-2. Because the Media Center options are designed to be accessed by using a special Media Center remote control (included with many Media Center PCs and with some brands of Media

Center TV tuner cards) as well as with a standard computer mouse, its interface is much more fluid than what you would find in other conventional Windows application windows (including the Windows Media Player) and dialog boxes.

Figure 6-2

The first thing you notice about the Media Center interface is the amount of audio and visual feedback it provides. At the time you launch the program and each time you select a menu option thereafter, Windows provides you with distinctive (and fairly harmonious) tones and clicks as well as visual clues to let you know which menu option you're about to select and when you've actually selected it.

The next thing to note is how easily you can cycle up and down through the main menu options either by positioning the mouse pointer on the up and down arrowheads (which look like white greater-than and less-than symbols rotated 90 degrees) or, if your mouse has a center wheel, by rolling it forward and backward to speed (and I do mean speed) through them. After you've highlighted the option you want, you can select it and display its submenu options by clicking the mouse button.

If you're using the Media Center remote control, you move up and down through the main menu options by pressing the device's up and down arrowheads (the black triangles pointing up and down). Click the OK button in the center of the remote (separating these arrowheads) to select the main option you want.

The Media Center's main menu options include

    ✔ **Extras,** used to access the Extras Library where you can play your favorite games on the computer or access the Extras Gallery, where you can sign up for special online services such as HSN Vision (to shop online), XM Radio Online (to listen to commercial-free radio), or CinemaNow (to order and download movies, TV shows, and music videos).

✔ **Pictures + Videos,** used to access the digital photos that are stored in your Pictures library (which you can then view as a slide show) or to access the video files in your Videos library (which you can then play in the Media Center window).

✔ **Music,** used to access your Music library and play tunes saved in it or to listen to your favorite Internet radio stations.

✔ **TV,** used to access live TV, recorded TV, and the online TV guide (if your computer has a TV tuner card and is connected to a cable or satellite dish).

✔ **Movies,** used to play movies on DVD that you've inserted into your computer's DVD drive; to get a listing of all the movies currently playing (assuming that you have a TV tuner card in your computer); or to search for movies on your computer by title, actor, or director.

✔ **Sports,** used to get the current and final scores for recent games involving your favorite sports teams as well as a schedule of upcoming televised sporting events.

✔ **Tasks,** used to burn media files stored on your computer's hard drive to a CD or DVD (assuming that your computer has DVD recording capabilities), synchronize media between your computer and another device connected to it, shut down the Media Center, or add the Media Center Extender or Media Center Extender for Xbox and to change your Media Center settings.

When you select the main menu option you want in the vertical listing, Media Center lists its submenu options horizontally. To view more submenu options, move the mouse pointer to the right, highlighting each one as you go, and then click to select the one you want to use.

If you're using the Media Center remote control, press the right arrowhead key (with the black triangle pointing to the right) to highlight each option in succession and then click the OK button to select the one you want to use.

Some submenu options lead to yet further levels of submenu options. Keep in mind, however, that you can always return to the previous level — all the way back to the main menu, if you so desire — by clicking the Back button (the black arrow pointing left that appears in a bar at the top of the Media Center window whenever you position the mouse pointer in this vicinity) or by pressing the Back button (which is labeled and uses the same black left-pointing arrow) when using the Media Center remote control.

If you regularly use the Media Center to play music, view your photos, and play your videos, consider adding the Windows Media Center gadget to your Windows 7 desktop (*see* "Gadgets" in Part 1 for details). This gadget enables you to open a slide show of the photos in your galleries (with or without a music background) in a Media Center window simply by clicking the Pictures or the Music + Pictures option. You can also set up this gadget so that it displays links to your favorite recorded TV videos saved on your computer or Internet TV videos on the Web.

When it's TV time

Who needs a separate TV when the Media Center is completely capable of playing your favorite TV shows right on your computer's fancy, new, 20-inch flat-panel display? You can watch Internet TV that downloads or streams snippets from recorded TV shows on the Web as well as live TV that's being transmitted by any of the seemingly millions of TV stations.

To be able to watch live TV in Windows's Media Center, your computer has to be equipped with a TV tuner card and hooked up either to your local cable system or to a satellite TV dish. Then, to set up Windows Media Center itself for live TV viewing, follow these steps:

1. Launch the Media Center by choosing Start⇨All Programs⇨Windows Media Center.

   Press the green button (sporting the Windows four-color flag logo) on the Media Center remote control.

2. Highlight TV on the Media Center main menu and then click the Live TV Setup option and follow the prompts to find your TV tuner card and select your TV provider. If you want, you can also subscribe and have the Windows Media Center download the Media Guide for your local area and TV provider.

After you set up the Windows Media Center for live TV, you can watch your favorite program on your computer by following these steps:

1. Launch the Windows Media Center and then highlight TV on the Media Center main menu and click the Live TV option.

   Press the Live TV button on the Media Center remote.

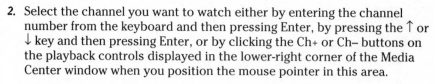

2. Select the channel you want to watch either by entering the channel number from the keyboard and then pressing Enter, by pressing the ↑ or ↓ key and then pressing Enter, or by clicking the Ch+ or Ch– buttons on the playback controls displayed in the lower-right corner of the Media Center window when you position the mouse pointer in this area.

   Use the numeric keypad to type in the channel number.

3. To adjust the volume, click the plus (+) or minus (–) buttons that appear to the right of the speaker icon on the playback controls displayed in the lower-right corner of the Media Center window when you position the mouse pointer in this area.

   Click the plus (+) or minus (–) pad of the button marked Vol on the Media Center remote.

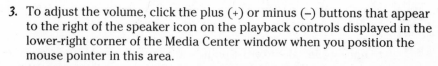

4. (Optional) To record the show you're watching, click the Record button on the playback controls displayed in the lower-right corner of the Media Center window.

Click the Record button on the Media Center remote.

Selecting live TV programs to record

Instead of recording TV programs as you're watching them, you can use your TV guide to schedule recording ahead of time. That way, not only can you watch them whenever you want to, but you can also use the Skip button (the one with the triangle pointing right against a vertical bar) either on the Media Center's playback controls or on the Media Center remote control to skip over all those annoying commercials.

To have the Windows Media Center record a program, follow these steps:

1. Launch the Media Center by choosing Start⇨All Programs⇨Windows Media Center.

Press the green button (sporting the Windows four-color flag logo) on the Media Center remote control.

2. Highlight TV on the Media Center main menu and then click the Guide option to display the online TV guide where you can select the program to record.

Press the Guide button on the Media Center remote.

3. Use the arrow keys on the keyboard to select the time and channel of a program playing sometime later in the day that you want the Media Center to record in the onscreen TV guide.

4. Press the Enter key to display a Program Info screen and then click its Record button — note that the program now displays a red dot in the TV guide indicating that it will be recorded.

Press the Record button on the Media Center remote.

If you want the Media Center to record all episodes of the show you've selected, click the Record Series button on the Program Info Media Center screen rather than the Record button.

TIP ➤ If you decide that you don't want to record one of the programs that you've selected for recording, click the program in the onscreen TV Guide and then click the Do Not Record button in the Program Info screen.

Watching recorded programs

After recording live TV programs onto your computer's hard drive, you can use the Media Center to play them back any time you want. To play your programs, launch the Media Center, highlight TV, and then click Recorded TV (or press the

Recorded TV button if your Media Center remote control has this button) to open the Recorded TV screen in the Media Center.

To play one of the recorded TV programs, click its thumbnail, press the Enter key to open its Program Info screen, and then click its Play button.

The Media Center automatically deletes recorded programs according to the Keep Until settings (often a particular date or until the disk space is needed). To prevent Media Center from deleting a recorded program that you haven't yet seen, click the Keep Until button in the Program Info screen and then click the Keep Until I Watch or Keep Until I Delete items.

Watching Internet TV

Even if your computer isn't equipped with a TV tuner card, that doesn't mean you can watch TV on your computer. Instead of live TV or live programs you've recorded, you can watch Internet TV in the Media Center, consisting of recorded clips from your favorite TV shows, sports events, music videos, and movie trailers that are downloaded from the Web.

To watch Internet TV, launch the Windows Media Center and then open the Guide in its TV section. In the Guide, select the thumbnail for the type of program you want to see by clicking it. (When you don't set up the Guide for live TV, the Guide displays thumbnails for each of the available Internet channels arranged by category, as shown in Figure 6-3.)

Figure 6-3

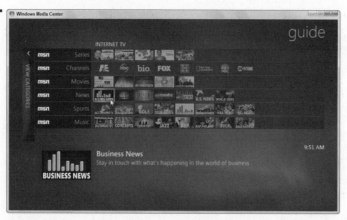

After you click a thumbnail for a particular Internet TV channel (such as Business News, in Figure 6-3), the Media Center displays a filmstrip of video clips that are available for viewing. (See Figure 6-4.) To view a particular clip, click its thumbnail in the filmstrip and then click the Play button that appears in its Synopsis box that contains a description of the clip along with its total running time.

To display the playback and volume controls in the Media Center window when viewing a video clip, position the mouse pointer near the bottom of the Media Center window. You can then use these controls to pause and restart the playback of the video as well as to adjust its volume. You can even go back and forth between the clip and the original Media Guide screen (by clicking Guide button, second from the left with the icon of a menu).

 If you click this Guide button to return to the original Media Guide screen without first pausing the playback of the video clip you're viewing, keep in mind that the video will continue to play in the background of the screen showing the table of channel icons. If you click the Back button in the upper-left corner of the Media Center window to return to the filmstrip of clips for the selected category, the currently viewed clip also continues to play in a thumbnail that appears in the lower-left corner of the window beneath the filmstrip.

Figure 6-4

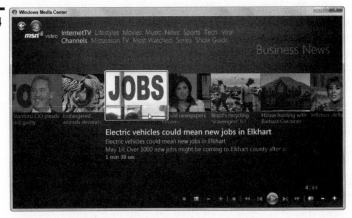

Playing your favorite tunes

You can use the Windows Media Center rather than the Windows Media Player (*see* "Windows Media Player" later in this part) to play the music you've stored on your computer's hard drive. To do play your music, launch the Windows Media Center and then choose Music⇨Music Library (or press the Music button on the Media Center remote control) to open the Music library screen in the Media Center.

To play a song, click its album thumbnail in the Music library screen. To play all the tracks on the album, click the Play Album button in the Album Details screen. To play a single track from the album, click its name and then click the Add to Now Playing button or the Play Song button in the onscreen playback controls.

 If you want to display a visualization of the music that you're playing in the Media Center, click the Visualize button. You can then cycle through the various visualizations available on your computer by pressing the → and ← on your keyboard or the Ch+ or Ch– button on your Media remote.

Playing your movies on DVD

The Windows Media Center (as well as the Windows Media Player discussed later in this part) can play movies stored on DVD — either those that you create with the Windows DVD Maker (*see* "Windows DVD Maker" later in this part for details) or professionally produced DVDs that you purchase or rent.

To play a DVD with the Windows Media Center, insert the DVD you want to play in your DVD drive. Launch the Windows Media Center and then choose Movies⇨Play DVD (or press the DVD Menu button on the Media Center remote control) to open the DVD's main menu, where you can then select the option you want, such as Chapter List, Language Selection, Bonus Materials, Play or Play Movie, and the like.

Click the Pause button if you need to temporarily pause the playback of the movie. If you click the Stop button on Media Center playback controls or press it on the remote control, the Media Center displays a screen of options, including Resume (to resume the movie from the frame where you selected Stop), Restart (to restart the movie from the beginning), and Eject (to open the DVD drive so you can remove the disc).

Viewing your preferred photos and videos

You can use the Windows Media Center to view the digital photos you store on your computer as well as to play back your videos. To view your photos, launch Media Center and then choose Pictures + Videos⇨Picture Library (or press the Pictures button on the Media Center remote control).

The Media Center then displays all the digital photos it has catalogued in your Pictures library by date. To display the photos in a particular folder added to your Pictures library, click its thumbnail in the Media Center window. Figure 6-5 shows you the photos stored in a folder called South America in the Pictures folder on my hard drive as they appear in my Pictures library in the Windows Media Center.

Figure 6-5

To scroll quickly (and I do mean, quickly) through the photos, position the mouse pointer on the left or right edge of the screen with the displayed thumbnails. A < or > symbol appears on the screen as you fly through the thumbnails. When you locate the thumbnail of a photo you want to view full size in the Pictures library screen or an image that you want to be the first in a slide show, click its thumbnail. To manually scroll through the photos, press the → or ← key. To start a slide show that automatically scrolls through each of the images one after the other, click the Play button in the onscreen playback controls. (You can also start a slide show from the very first photo by clicking the Play Slide Show link in the Pictures library.)

If you want to play a video you've stored on your computer rather than view photos, all you need to do is open the Videos library by choosing Pictures + Videos⇨Video Library from the Windows Media Center Start screen (or by pressing the Videos button on the Media Center remote control). To play a video in the library, you simply open its folder and then click its thumbnail in the gallery (see Figure 6-6).

Figure 6-6

Windows DVD Maker

The Windows DVD Maker program included with Windows 7 enables you to burn video DVDs by using digital photos or videos you've saved on your computer that you can then play back in standalone DVD players connected to a TV. Best of all, this handy little program lets you create menus for your video DVD just like those created for professional movies released on DVD for purchase or rent. All you need is a blank DVD and a DVD drive on your computer that's capable of writing DVDs.

To create a new video DVD with Windows DVD Maker, follow these steps:

1. Insert a blank DVD into your computer's DVD drive.

2. Choose Start⇨All Programs⇨Windows DVD Maker to launch Windows DVD Maker.

3. (Optional) If the Share Your Memories on a DVD start screen appears (because you didn't deselect the Don't Show This Page Again check box), you must click the Choose Photos and Videos button in the initial Windows DVD Maker window to open the Add Pictures and Video to the DVD screen.

4. Click the Add Items button on the Windows DVD Maker window's toolbar to display the Open dialog box.

5. Select all the digital videos you want to add to your DVD by clicking the appropriate media folder in the Favorite Links section of the Navigation pane and then selecting their file icons before you click Open.

    Hold down the Ctrl key and click individual icons to select multiple video files for the DVD.

6. Replace the title that automatically appears in the DVD Title text box in the lower-right corner of the Windows DVD Maker window — it uses the current date — with a title that you want to appear on the DVD menu.

7. (Optional) After selecting all the video files for the DVD, select the video thumbnail and then use the Move Up or Move Down button to modify the order in which they automatically play on the DVD.

8. (Optional) Click the Options link to the immediate right of the Disc Title text box to open the DVD-Video Options dialog box, and then make any necessary changes to how the DVD plays — its aspect ratio (4:3 or 16:9), for example, or its video format (NTSC or PAL) — before you click OK.

    If you're making the DVD for a DVD player sold in the United States, you don't need to change the Video Format option from NTSC to PAL.

9. Click Next to open the Ready to Burn to DVD screen in the Windows DVD Maker window. (See Figure 6-7.)

10. Click the thumbnail with the type of menu style you want your DVD to use in the Menu Styles list box on the right side of Windows DVD Maker window.

    Note that you can click the Menu Text button to customize the text that appears on the buttons used by the menu style you select. You can also click the Customize button if you want to modify certain aspects of the menu style, including adding a foreground or background video as well as a menu audio track that plays until the user selects one of the menu options.

11. (Optional) Click the Preview button on the Windows DVD Maker window's toolbar to preview it and then, after experimenting with the menu and previewing your video content, click OK.

12. Click the Burn button below the Menu Styles list box to start burning your videos to the DVD.

Figure 6-7

After you click Burn, a Creating DVD dialog box appears, which keeps you informed of the progress of the burn. After the entire project is burned to disc, the Your Disc Is Ready dialog box appears, and Windows DVD Maker automatically ejects the DVD.

If you want to make another copy of the DVD, replace the ejected disc with a new blank disc and then click the Duplicate This Disc link in the Your Disc Is Ready dialog box. If you don't want to make another copy, remove the ejected disc, close the DVD drive door, and then click the Close button in the dialog box instead.

TIP

When using Windows DVD Maker to create a slide show of a selection of your digital photos, click the Slide Show button on the Windows DVD Maker window's toolbar so that you can customize the number of seconds each photo in the slide show is displayed, the type of transition to use when going from one image to another, and to add any background music you want playing during the show.

Windows Media Player

You can use Windows Media Player 12 to play audio, video, and animation files that you either save on your computer or (if you have a fast connection to the Internet, also known as *broadband*) play online as they're being downloaded to your computer (a technique known as *streaming*). You can use Windows Media Player to play Internet radio stations, as well as to view video clips from Internet TV. Of course, the most important thing is that Windows Media Player also plays all the MP3 (short for MPEG3, which is a compression scheme developed by the motion picture entertainment industry) audio files that you've downloaded from your favorite music Web sites, including the most recent additions to Napster, eMusic, Rhapsody, and all the rest.

To launch the Windows Media Player, click the Windows Media Player button (the third button from the Start button with the triangle pointing to the right inside an orange circle) on the Windows 7 taskbar or choose Start➪All Programs➪ Windows Media Player. You're able to use Windows Media Player in one of three window views:

✔ **Library view** (Ctrl+1), the default view shown in Figure 6-8, where you can manage your media as well as choose the music, photo, or video for playback with the Windows Media Player.

✔ **Skin view** (Ctrl+2), shown in Figure 6-9, where you view the video or music playback in the *skin* — the container or border — that either comes with Windows 7 or is one that you've download from the Internet. (In the case of music, you "view" the playback using one of the visualizations you either downloaded from the Internet or already had as part of Windows 7.)

✔ **Now Playing view** (Ctrl+3), shown in Figure 6-10, where you can view the video or play the music in a standard window. (Again, in the case of music, you "view" the playback using either one of the default visualizations or a visualization you've downloaded from the Internet.)

TIP

Even after minimizing the Media Player window to just the Windows Media Player button on the Windows 7 taskbar, you can still control the playback of the music or video you were enjoying. Simply position the mouse pointer over the Windows Media Player button on the taskbar and then click the Pause or Play (depending on the current state of the playback) displayed in the thumbnail that appears above this button on the taskbar.

Figure 6-8

Figure 6-9

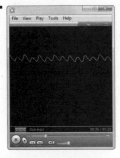

Figure 6-10

Keep in mind that you can also play music or watch videos in full-screen mode by pressing Alt+Enter or by clicking the View Full Screen button in the lower-right corner when you're viewing the Windows Media Player in Now Playing mode. In full-screen mode, the music visualization or video takes up the entire screen except for a bar at the bottom that contains the playback controls and an Exit Full-Screen Mode button on the far right. (Note that this bar disappears during playback and remains hidden until you position the mouse pointer near the bottom of the screen.)

Using the Windows Media Player in Library view

When you launch the Windows Media Player in the default Library view (refer to Figure 6-8), you can easily select the media you want for playback. Simply click the media category under Library in the window's Navigation pane (Playlists, Music, Videos, Pictures, or Recorded TV). The Windows Media Player then displays a list of so-called *tiles* (thumbs plus information) for all the various playlists, albums, video clips, or photos currently added to the media libraries on your computer.

To select a particular media item for playback, simply selects its tile in the center of the Media Player and then click the Play button in the center of the controls that appear at the bottom of the Media Player window. In the case of albums in your Music library, you can play a particular track in an album by clicking the track name in the list followed by the Play button. To play back the entire album, click the link attached to the album's title right next to the album cover picture before you click the Play button.

To change the contents of a particular media library, display the pull-down menus (by pressing Ctrl+M) and then select File⇨Manage Libraries followed by the name of the library (Music, Videos, Pictures, or Recorded TV). Windows then opens the Locations dialog box for the particular library you selected. This Locations dialog box shows you all the folders that Windows currently looks in for the files of the particular media type. To add other folders, click the Add button and then select the folder(s) to include in the Include Folder dialog box.

Using the Media Guide

The Navigation pane of the Windows Media Player in the default Library view contains a Media Guide button that you can click to get access to all types of various media files and clips on the Internet. These media files include music videos of the latest song releases, video clips for the latest TV shows, movie trailers, and top news stories as well as video games and online radio stations whose music you can play with the Windows Media Player.

When you select the Media Guide button, the Media Player displays the Media Guide to the right of the Navigation pane. Here, you can select the type of media you're interested in by clicking its link (Music, Movies, or TV) at the top of the display. To play a particular clip or song in the Media Player, click its picture in the Media Guide.

Keep in mind that, when you select a video clip or music video in the Media Guide fro playback, the Media Player usually plays the video in its Now Playing view. After the video finishes playing, you can then return to the default Library view by clicking the Switch to Library button — the one labeled Go to Library with the icon with three little squares and an arrowhead pointing to the left that appears in the center of the Now Playing Media Player window.

Creating playlists

You can easily create playlists that determine the playback order for music, photos, or videos you want to play in the Media Player. The only trick to doing creating playlists is that you must first display the List pane in the Media Player when it's in Library view by choosing Organize⇨Layout⇨Show List.

To select the music, photos, or videos that you want the playlist to play in the Media Player, simply drag its icon to List pane (in the area that says Drag Items Here). After you finish adding all the media items you want to the playlist, you save the playlist by clicking the Save List button above the List pane, typing a descriptive name for the new playlist, and then pressing the Enter key.

After creating a playlist, you can play back its media items simply by launching the Windows Media Library, locating the playlist in the Playlists section of the Navigation pane and then double-clicking the playlist name.

You can edit the contents of a playlist at any time after creating it. To remove a song from the list, right-click it and then choose Remove From List from the shortcut menu that appears. To change the order of a song in the list, right-click it and then choose Move Up or Move Down from its shortcut menu as needed to get it into the desired position in the list. To add a new song to the playlist, drag its icon from the Navigation pane of the Media Player and drop it at the desired position in the List pane.

Ripping and burning CDs

You can use the Rip CD button on the Windows Media Player toolbar to rip tracks from audio CDs you own for playback on your computer or on a compatible portable MP3 player. Likewise, you can use its Burn button to burn tracks to a blank CD.

To rip tracks from an audio CD and save them on your computer's hard drive, insert the audio CD into your computer's CD/DVD drive, and then click the Rip CD button on the toolbar. The Media Player then begins ripping the tracks, showing the status for each track as well as displaying a progress bar for the track currently being ripped (see Figure 6-11).

Figure 6-11

The Media Player automatically copies all tracks in the Windows Media Audio (.wma) file format. To rip tracks using the more compressed MP3 file format, you need to choose Rip Settings➪Format➪MP3 from the Windows Media Player main menu before you insert the audio CD in the computer's drive. To rip only some of the tracks from a CD, deselect the check marks from the tracks that you don't want copied from the audio CD to your Music library.

After ripping the tracks from a CD album, Windows automatically adds the album to its Music section. You can then play its tracks or add some or all of them to a new or existing playlist by selecting the album in the Music section of the Navigation pane and displaying a list of their tracks in the Media Player.

To burn tracks to a blank CD, insert the blank audio CD in your computer's CD/DVD drive and then click the Burn button on the Media Player toolbar. The Media Player then displays a Burn List in the List pane, where you assemble the tracks you want to copy to a blank CD by dragging their album and song icons from the Media Library or by dragging their playlists and then dropping them onto the Drag Items Here section.

After you've assembled all the tracks in the order in which you want them copied in the Burn List, click the Start Burn button at the bottom of the List pane in the Media Player. The Windows Media Player then burns all the tracks you've added to the Burn List onto the blank audio CD. When all the tracks have been successfully copied, the Media Player then automatically ejects the disc from the CD/DVD drive (which you then should immediately label before you put it away in a CD sleeve or plastic case).

Synching up with a portable MP3 player

If you own a compatible portable MP3 player or music-enabled cellphone, you can synchronize the music files (as well as photos and videos, if your device can display and play them) in your Windows Media Library with the portable device.

To do get syncing, first connect your portable device to the computer running Windows 7 and then, if a dialog box asking you to sync with Windows Media Player doesn't automatically appear, launch the Windows Media Player and then click the Sync button on its toolbar. Next, drag all the media files (including playlists) you want to copy onto the portable playback device from the main area of the Media Player to the Sync List in the pane on the right, and then, finally, click the Start Sync button at the top of the pane. (See Figure 6-12.)

Sync button

Figure 6-12

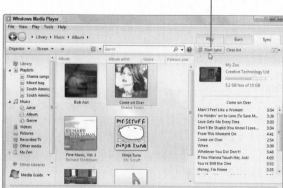

The Windows Media Player then shows you the progress on synchronizing each file. To stop the synchronization before all the files you added to the Sync List are copied, click the Stop Sync button. When Media Player finishes synchronizing all the files added to the Sync List, it then displays the free space left on your portable device at the top of the right-hand pane.

After the Windows Media Player finishes synchronizing your media files, you can verify that they've been transferred to the portable device by expanding its listing in the Navigation pane and then selecting the type of media (Music, Video, or Pictures) that you want displayed in the Media Player window.

Accessories

Windows 7 comes with a whole bunch of specialized utilities — referred to collectively as *accessories* — that can help you do work on the computer. These accessories run the gamut from a simple Calculator for quick math computations all the way to WordPad, a slimmed-down word processor for composing simple documents. This part introduces you to some of the more commonly used Windows 7 accessories. As the following figure shows, in Windows 7, all accessories are grouped together on the Start menu in an Accessories subfolder. To use an accessory, all you do is choose Start⇨All Programs⇨Accessories and then click the name of the particular accessory you want to launch.

In this part . . .

✔ **Using Command Prompt and Run to Do DOS-Type Stuff**

✔ **Using Notepad, Paint, and WordPad to Create Simple Documents**

✔ **Using the Snipping Tool and Sticky Notes to Capture Ideas**

Calculator

The Calculator is a nifty tool designed for doing all kinds of quick calculations. When you first open the calculator (Start@⇨All Programs⇨Accessories⇨Calculator), the standard, basic Calculator window appears (similar to the one shown in Figure 7-1). With the Calculator in standard mode and with the basic configuration, you can do simple mathematical operations by entering the values to be computed separated by the operator (+ for addition, – for subtraction, * for multiplication, and / for division) and then clicking the equal (=) key.

Figure 7-1

Keep in mind that you can enter your numbers and mathematical operators into the Windows Calculator directly from the keyboard using its number keys or numeric keypad rather than always clicking the numbers and operation symbol buttons in the Calculator window.

When using the Calculator, you're not restricted to using the accessory in its default standard mode. The Calculator also offers the following computation modes that you can switch to by choosing the following menu options on its View menu (or pressing the shortcut keys shown in parentheses):

- **Scientific (Alt+2):** Adds keys for performing trigonometric calculations — great for all the engineers out there.

- **Programmer (Alt+3):** Adds keys for performing programming calculations in different number systems, including hexadecimal, octal, and binary number systems, along with the usual decimal system using different word and byte sizes (and if you don't know what that is, you probably don't need this mode).

- **Statistics (Alt+4):** Adds keys for doing statistical calculations involving linear regression.

In addition to the basic configuration — perfect for doing straightforward computations — the Calculator also offers the following specialized configurations (also available from the View menu) designed for more complex calculations:

- 🗸 **Unit Conversion (Ctrl+U):** Adds fields for converting all sorts of measurements (angles, pressures, temperatures, weights, time, velocities, mass, and so on) from one set of units to another.

- 🗸 **Date Calculation (Ctrl+E):** Adds fields for performing calculations between two dates.

- 🗸 **Worksheets:** Adds fields for calculating results, such as finding the necessary down payment or your monthly mortgage payment using the Mortgage option; the monthly lease payment or residual value of a leased vehicle using the Vehicle Lease option; or the fuel economy of your vehicle using the Fuel Economy (mpg) option for miles per gallon or the Fuel Economy (L/100 km) option for liters per hundred kilometers.

Press Alt+1 to return the Calculator immediately to standard mode from any of the other three modes and press Ctrl+F4 to return to the basic configuration from any of the other available configurations.

Command Prompt

You use the Command Prompt accessory (Start➪All Programs➪Accessories➪ Command Prompt) to open a Command Prompt window like the one shown in Figure 7-2. This window contains the old (and I do mean *old*) DOS command prompt (the flashing cursor shown on the last line in the figure), where you can directly run computer system commands (if you know any) by typing them in at the prompt and then pressing the Enter key.

To get help on available system commands, type **help** at the command prompt and press Enter. To get sparse (and I do mean sparse) help on a particular system command, type **help** followed by a forward slash (/) and the name of the system command. For example, to get help on using the ipconfig system command, enter the following at the command prompt:

```
help /ipconfig
```

Figure 7-2

A few system commands require that you open the Command Prompt window as an administrator before you can enter it. To run the Command Prompt accessory as an administrator (assuming that your user account is so rated), choose Start⇨All Programs⇨Accessories and then right-click Command Prompt to display its shortcut menu. There, click the Run as Administrator item near the top and then click the Yes button in the User Account Control alert dialog box to open the Administrator: Command Prompt window.

Notepad

You can use the Notepad accessory (Start⇨All Programs⇨Accessories⇨Notepad), shown in Figure 7-3, to open and edit text files. Notepad is perfect for editing and printing text files (notably, HTML files, if you don't have access to any other dedicated Web Page editors . . . and know how to edit HTML tags).

In Notepad, the File menu provides you with the following commands, which are essential for editing text files:

- ✔ **New** to start a new text file

- ✔ **Open** to an existing text file for editing

- ✔ **Save** and **Save As** to save changes to the text file you're editing

- ✔ **Page Setup** to modify the page settings for printing the text file you're editing, including the paper size, source, orientation, margins, and header and footer

- ✔ **Print** to print a hard copy of the text file you're editing

Figure 7-3

```
Home Page - Notepad
File   Edit   Format   View   Help
<!DOCTYPE HTML PUBLIC "-//W3C//DTD HTML 4.0 Transitional//EN">
<!-- saved from url=(0029)http://www.mindovermedia.com/ -->
<HTML><HEAD><TITLE>Home Page</TITLE>
<META http-equiv=Content-Language content=en-us>
<META http-equiv=Content-Type content="text/html; charset=windows-1252">
<META content="Microsoft FrontPage 5.0" name=GENERATOR>
<META content=FrontPage.Editor.Document name=ProgId>
<META content="profile-souped-up 011" name="Microsoft Theme">
<META content="tlb, default" name="Microsoft Border"></HEAD>
<BODY text=#000000 vLink=#666666 aLink=#ff0000 link=#990033 bgcolor=#ffcc66
background="Home Page_files/probkgnd.gif">
       <P><IMG height=93 src="Home Page_files/momtrdmk.gif" width=249 align=left
       border=0></P>
       <P>welcome to Mind Over Media, web site for author Greg Harvey. <BR>2005
       marks the 22nd anniversary since he wrote his first computer book. In
       these intervening years, he's not only seen computers change from being
       primarily expensive "calculators" to becoming rather inexpensive and
       highly sophisticated "communication" devices.</P>
       <P>2005 has been another busy year for Mind Over Media. This is the year
       that Greg has finally finished graduate school, receiving his Ph.D. in
       Philosophy and Religion  </P>
       <P>In 2003, Greg  ad the great opportunity to write his first
       non-computer book:<BR><I>The Origins of Tolkien's Middle-earth For
       Dummies</I>, which explores some of the mythological and etymological
       origins of J.R.R. Tolkien's fantasy world and also examines some of its
       important themes. To celebrate the publishing of this book and to help his readers use
       it, Greg has put together an interactive Middle-earth glossary in PDF
       format with internal links to cross-referenced items and external links to
       wonderful new Middle-earth maps prepared by Melinda Bryant (click <A
       href="http://www.mindovermedia.com/me_goodies.htm">Middle-earth
       Goodies</A> or the Middle-earth Goodies button in the left panel to see
       this glossary).</P>

</BODY></HTML>
```

Because text files don't generally require any fancy formatting, Notepad includes only two options on its Format menu: Word Wrap to wrap lines of text to the current margins set for the text file and Font to modify the font, style, and font size (Lucida Console, Regular, 10-point) to something a little more stylish. If your document requires formatting changes any more elaborate than this, you need to use the WordPad accessory, rather than Notepad. (*See* "WordPad" later in this part for details.)

Paint

The Paint accessory (Start➪All Programs➪Accessories➪Paint), shown in Figure 7-4, provides you with a simple program for creating and editing the graphics files you work with. You can use Paint to create new graphics or to edit existing ones. The program offers you a number of brush, line, and fill tools that you can use when drawing a new image or touching up an existing one.

The Paint accessory can open graphics saved in a variety of different image formats (including bitmap, JPEG, GIF, TIFF, and PNG). The program can also save the images that you create or touch up with in these different formats. To open a graphics file for editing in Paint, click the Paint button (the one to the immediate left of the Home tab at the top of the window) and then choose Open from its drop-down menu.

Figure 7-4

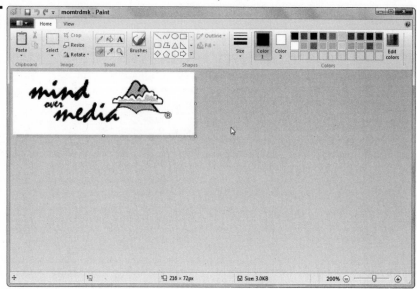

To save the file you've been editing with Paint in a new graphics file format, click the Paint button and then choose Save As from the drop-down menu. A submenu opens, offering a choice of the following graphics file formats: PNG Picture, JPEG Picture, BMP Picture, and GIF Picture. To save the image in a file format other than one of these four, click the Other Formats option at the bottom of this submenu and then select the graphics format from the Save As Type drop-down list in the Save As dialog box.

Don't confuse Paint's abilities to edit graphics in a digital photo with the photo-editing abilities of a dedicated photo-editing program such as Windows Live Photo Editor. A dedicated photo-editing program includes features for adjusting the picture's overall quality (in terms of exposure, brightness, contrast, filters, and the tint and color saturation) and formatting (in terms of cropping, rotating, and straightening the image) that are totally lacking in Paint.

Run

You use the Run accessory (Start⇨All Programs⇨Accessories⇨Run), shown in Figure 7-5, to launch programs or even open documents that, for whatever reason, fail to open automatically using the Windows 7 AutoRun feature. (The Run accessory is especially good for running setup programs stored on CDs or DVDs that fail to automatically run.)

Figure 7-5

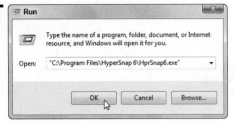

To launch a program from the Run window, type its location (including the drive letter and folder path) in the Open text box and then click OK. If you don't know the path, click the Browse button and display the folder containing the program file in the Browse dialog box before you click Open.

If you're trying to open a document file with the Run accessory, you need to open the Browse dialog box. Select All Files from the drop-down list to the right of its File Name text box and then select the file and click Open. After you click OK in the Run window, Windows opens an Open With dialog box where you need to select the program you want to use to open the document before you click OK.

Snipping Tool

The Snipping Tool accessory (Start⇨All Programs⇨Accessories⇨Snipping Tool), illustrated in Figure 7-6, enables you to quickly capture a portion of the text and graphics you have displayed onscreen. After you use the accessory to capture a snippet (usually from a favorite Website), you can then save it as a graphics file, copy it into the Window Clipboard for pasting into a document, or even send it to someone as an e-mail attachment.

To snip a portion of a Web page, open the page in the Internet Explorer 8 and then launch the Snipping Tool from the Windows Start menu. When you first open the Snipping Tool, Windows 7 dims its desktop and opens the accessory in a small dialog box.

You then use the white-cross mouse pointer that appears on the screen to drag an outline around the area of the Web page you want to capture. After you release the mouse button, Windows reopens the Snipping Tool window, this time containing the text and graphics you selected in the Web page. You can then use the Snipping Tools buttons or menus to save the image in a file, copy it to the Clipboard, or send it in an e-mail.

Figure 7-6

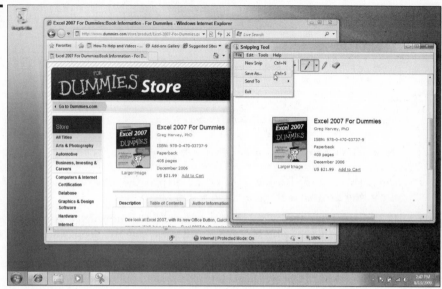

Sound Recorder

The Sound Recorder accessory (Start⇨All Programs⇨Accessories⇨Sound Recorder), shown in Figure 7-7, enables you to record sounds via your computer's built-in microphone or one that you've connected to its microphone jack (perhaps to dictate text or give voice commands using Windows 7 Speech Recognition — *see* "Speech Recognition" in Part 4 for details).

Figure 7-7

When you first open the Sound Recorder, it contains a Start Recording button with a red dot that you click when you want to start recording with your microphone. When you finish your sound recording, you then click the Stop Recording button with the green square (that replaces the Start Recording button).

The moment you click the Stop Recording button, the Save As dialog box opens, prompting you to save the recording you just made as a Windows Media Audio file. To save the recording, type a name in the File Name text box, select the folder in which you want to save the recording, and then click Save.

Sticky Notes

The Sticky Notes accessory (Start➪All Programs➪Accessories➪Sticky Notes) enables you to plaster the electronic equivalent of good old-fashioned Post-It notes all over your Windows 7 desktop. (See Figure 7-8 for a good example.)

Figure 7-8

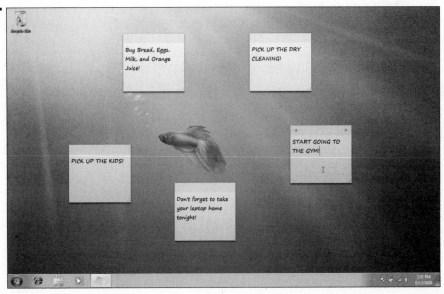

Sticky Notes make excellent onscreen reminders because they can't fall off like Post-Its do. They remain securely wherever you put them on the desktop until you delete them!

When you open Sticky Notes, Windows opens a new blank note on the desktop, positioning the cursor at the beginning of the note. You can then type the text of the note, which automatically wraps to a new line. Should your note run so long that its text goes beyond the end of the last line, Windows automatically expands the height of the note to accommodate a new line.

When you finish entering the note text, you can click the New Note button (the one with the plus sign) to start a new sticky note or, if you don't need to add any more notes, you can simply click somewhere on the desktop outside the sticky note itself.

To temporarily hide all the sticky notes that you've placed on the Windows 7 desktop, click the Sticky Notes Quick Launch button on the taskbar. When you open an Explorer window that overlaps a note, the window naturally obscures the sticky note. To bring the sticky note to the top of the desktop so that it sits on top of the open Explorer window, click a part of the sticky note's window (if it's visible). If none of the note window is visible, click the Sticky Notes Quick Launch button on the taskbar.

To delete a note that you no longer need, click its Delete button in the upper-right corner. The first time you delete a note, Windows displays a Sticky Notes alert dialog box where you need to confirm the deletion by clicking the Yes button. If you don't ever want to see this confirmation alert again, you need to select the Don't Display This Message Again check box before you click Yes.

You can color-code the sticky notes you add to the desktop: Simply right-click the note and then click the color you want for the background from the shortcut menu that appears. (Your choices here are Blue, Green, Pink, Purple, White, or Yellow.) If you want to enhance the note text a tad, you need to select it with the cursor and then press the appropriate shortcut key: Ctrl+B for bold text, Ctrl+I for italics, and Ctrl+U for underlining.

WordPad

The WordPad accessory (Start➪All Programs➪Accessories➪WordPad), shown in Figure 7-9, offers you very basic word processing. You can use WordPad to compose and print simple documents such as memos, letters, and the like.

Unlike the text editor accessory, Notepad, Windows 7 WordPad supports rudimentary paragraph formatting in the form of indents, bulleted and numbered lists, and Center, Right, and Justify paragraph text alignment along with text enhancement, such as new fonts, font sizes, and text effects (Bold, Italic, Underline, Strikethrough, Subscript, and Superscript). The program even supports the addition of graphics files such as photos to its text documents.

WordPad automatically saves its documents in Microsoft's .rtf (Rich Text File) file format, which full-fledged word-processing programs such as Microsoft Word can readily open. You can, however, save WordPad documents in other text file formats: Simply click the WordPad button, highlight Save As on its drop-down menu, and then select the new format on the submenu (Rich Text Document, Office Open XML Document, OpenDocument Text, or Plain Text Document).

Figure 7-9

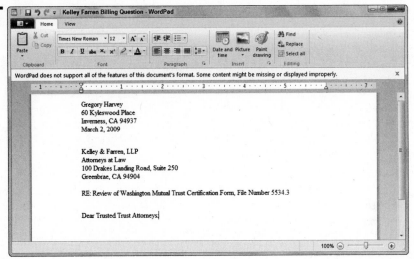

Windows Live Essentials

To streamline Windows 7 a little bit, the software engineers at Microsoft removed a whole host of useful applications (including Windows Mail, Movie Maker, and Photo Gallery) that were automatically installed in most editions of earlier Windows versions (especially that monster, Vista). However, just because these programs aren't automatically installed with Windows 7 doesn't mean you don't have access to them. If you need them, you can download them (for free) as part of the Essentials package from the Windows Live Web site shown in the following figure. Choose Start⇨Getting Started⇨Get Windows Live Essentials to open the Windows Live page in Internet Explorer 8 and then click the Download button.

In this part . . .

- ✏ Using Windows Live Mail to Send and Receive Your E-Mail
- ✏ Using Windows Live Messenger to Send and Receive Instant Messages
- ✏ Using Windows Live Movie Maker to Organize Your Video Clips
- ✏ Using Windows Live Photo Gallery to Organize Your Photos

Mail

If you don't have an e-mail program such as Microsoft Outlook already installed on your computer, you can download and use Windows Live Mail as your e-mail program. Not only does Windows Live Mail (shown in Figure 8-1) enable you to send and receive e-mail, but it also supports RSS feeds and newsgroups and contains a Calendar module (where you can keep your schedule of upcoming events) as well as a Contacts module (where you can store your e-mail contacts).

Figure 8-1

Information viewer

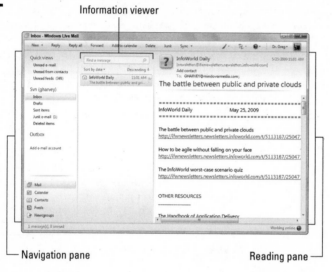

Navigation pane

Reading pane

As you can see in Figure 8-1, the Live Mail window is divided into three separate panes:

- **Navigation pane:** This left pane enables you to switch from mail to other functions including the calendar, contacts, RSS feeds, and newsgroups.

- **Information viewer:** This center pane lists the subject of each e-mail message you receive along with the date it's received and the first few words of the message.

- **Reading pane:** This pane displays the details of the e-mail that's selected in the Information viewer, including to whom and from whom the message is sent, the date and time it was sent, and all message text that can be displayed in the window. (Graphic images aren't automatically displayed with the text; you must click the Show Images link at the top of the pane to display them).

Creating a new e-mail account

After downloading Windows Live Mail (downloading it alone or with other applications in the Windows Live Essentials suite), the first time you launch the program (Start⇨All Programs⇨Windows Live⇨Windows Live Mail), the program leads you through the steps of setting up a new e-mail account. You can also set up a new account from within Windows Live Mail by following these steps:

1. Open Windows Live Mail by choosing Start⇨Windows Live⇨Windows Live Mail and then clicking the Add E-mail Account link in the Navigation pane.

   Windows Live Mail opens the Add an E-mail Account dialog box.

2. Enter your e-mail address in the E-mail Address text box.

3. Enter your password in the Password text box.

4. Enter your name in the Display Name text box and then click Next.

5. If your incoming e-mail server doesn't use the POP3 protocol, click IMAP on the My Incoming Mail Server Is a POP3 Server drop-down list box.

   Your ISP's mail server that sends your e-mail to the Windows Mail program uses one of two protocols: POP3 (Post Office Protocol version 3) or IMAP (Internet Message Access Protocol, also known as IMAP version 4), just as its mail server that receives the messages you send out through Windows Mail uses the SMTP (Simple Mail Transfer Protocol) protocol.

   Check with your ISP about the type of incoming server you use when you find out the names of the ISP's incoming and outgoing mail servers, which you'll also need to have on hand in order to set up an e-mail account.

6. Enter the name of your ISP's mail server in the Incoming Server text box.

7. Enter the name of the outgoing mail server in the Outgoing Server text box.

8. If your outgoing mail server requires you to enter a user ID and password, click the My Server Requires Authentication check box.

9. If you want to make the new e-mail account your default account in Windows Live Mail that's automatically used when you send a message from the Internet Explorer, select the Set This Account as the Default Mail Account check box.

10. Click the Finish button to return to the Windows Live Mail window.

After setting up a new e-mail account, the name of the mail account (with its own Inbox, Drafts, Sent Items, June E-Mail, and Deleted Items) appears in the Windows Live Mail Navigation pane.

Composing and sending messages

To compose and send a new e-mail message in Windows Live Mail, follow these steps:

1. Click the New button and then choose E-Mail Message from its drop-down menu or simply press Ctrl+N.

   Windows Live Mail opens the New Message window, where you specify the recipient's e-mail address in the To field (which automatically contains the cursor). You can either type this address in the To text box or click the To button to display the Select Contacts to Send E-Mail To dialog box, in which you can select the recipients from a list of contacts in your Contacts List or from one of the online directories.

   To send a new message to someone who's already listed in your Contacts List, click the Contacts button in the Windows Live Mail Navigation pane in the lower-left corner and then click the contact's name in the Windows Live Contacts window before you click the E-Mail button on the toolbar. Windows Live Mail then opens a New Message window, with the recipient's e-mail address already entered in the To field.

   When composing a new message, you can send copies of it to as many other recipients (within reason) as you want. To send copies of the message to other recipients, you first need to click the Show Cc and Bcc link to add the Cc and Bcc fields to the message.

2. (Optional) Click somewhere in the Cc field and then type the e-mail addresses, separated by semicolons (;) in the Cc field. Alternatively, if the addresses appear in the Contacts List, click the Cc button to open the Select Recipients dialog box and then choose the e-mail addresses there. (After clicking the names in the Name list box, click the Cc button to add them to the copy list.)

   After filling in the e-mail addresses of the recipients, you're ready to enter the subject of the message. The descriptive text that you type in the Subject field of the message appears in the upper pane of a recipient's Inbox when he or she reads the message.

3. Click somewhere in the Subject field and then enter a brief description of the contents or purpose of the e-mail message.

4. (Optional) To boost the priority of the message, click the High Priority button on the toolbar. To decrease the priority of the message, click the Low Priority button instead.

   When you make a message either high or low priority, Windows Live Mail attaches a priority icon to the message (assuming that the recipients of the message are using Windows Live Mail, Outlook Express, or Outlook to read their mail) that indicates its relative importance. The high-priority icon has a red flag in front of the envelope, whereas the low-priority icon has an arrow pointing downward.

5. Click in the body of the message and then type in the text of the message as you would in any text editor or word processor, ending paragraphs by pressing the Enter key.

   When composing the text of the message, keep in mind that you can insert text directly into the body of the message from other documents via the Clipboard (the old cut, copy, and paste commands).

6. (Optional) To send a file along with your e-mail, click the Attach button on the toolbar, select the file in the Open dialog box, and then click the Open button.

   When you include a file with a message, an icon for the file appears in a new Attach field between the Subject field and the body of the e-mail.

7. To send the e-mail to its recipients, click the Send button on the toolbar.

TIP Note that when composing a new message, you can send *blind copies* of the message to several recipients by filling in the Bcc field. When you add names to the Bcc (blind carbon copy) field rather than to the Cc (carbon copy) field, none of the Bcc recipients sees any other names you may have entered in the Bcc field. When you add names to the Cc field, each recipient sees the names of everyone else to whom you've sent this same message. To display the Bcc field between the Cc and Subject fields, click the Show Cc and Bcc link. You can fill in this field with the names of the recipients as you do in the Cc field. (***See*** Step 3 in the preceding list.)

Adding recipients to the Contact List

Windows Live Mail makes it easy to maintain an address book (referred to as Windows Live Contacts), where you can store the e-mail addresses for all the people you regularly correspond with. If you're switching from some other e-mail program (such as the one that comes with Netscape Navigator), and you've created an address book with that program, you can even import all the addresses into the Contacts List so you don't have to reenter them.

To add a new recipient to the Windows Live Contacts list, follow these steps:

1. Launch Windows Live Mail (Start➪All Programs➪Windows Live➪Windows Live Mail) and then click the Contacts button near the bottom of the Navigation pane (refer to Figure 8-1) to open the Windows Live Contacts window.

2. Click the New button on the Windows Live Contacts toolbar to open the Add a Contact dialog box.

3. Fill in the First Name and Last Name fields and then select the Personal E-Mail text box, where you type the recipient's e-mail address before adding the optional Home Phone and Company information.

4. (Optional) In the Add a Contact dialog box, click the Contact button in the Navigation pane and then add the work e-mail address in the Work E-Mail field and any alternative e-mail address in the Other E-Mail field.

   If you want to make the work or alternative personal e-mail address the default address that Windows Mail automatically uses when you compose a new message, you need to select Work or Other in the Primary E-Mail Address drop-down list when the Contact button is selected in the Add a Contact dialog box.

TIP

   To use a contact's work or alternative e-mail address in a new message, you need to click the To button in the new message and then select that e-mail address in the Select Contacts to Send E-Mail To dialog box.

5. (Optional) If you want to add other information about the contact, such as home and work contact information or personal notes, click the Contact button in the Add a Contact dialog box and fill in the appropriate fields.

6. Click the Add Contact button to close the Add a Contact dialog box.

   Windows Live Mail returns you to the Windows Live Contacts window, where an icon for the new contact appears. You can display the particulars, such as the name, e-mail address, business phone, and home phone displayed for any contact in the list by selecting his or her icon.

7. When you finish adding and modifying contacts in the Windows Live Contacts window, close it by clicking its Close button.

To import the addresses from an existing address book created with Eudora, Microsoft Exchange, Microsoft Internet Mail for Windows, Outlook Express, Outlook, or Netscape Navigator into the Contact List, or to import addresses stored in a comma-separated text file, follow these steps:

1. Launch Windows Live Mail (Start⇨All Programs⇨Windows Live⇨Windows Live Mail) and then open the Windows Live Contacts window by clicking the Contacts button in its Navigation pane.

2. Click the Menus drop-down button on the toolbar — the button on the right side of the bar to the immediate left of the Help button.

3. Highlight the Import item on the Menus drop-down menu and then select the type of address book file you want to import in the list box on the submenu: Windows Address Book (.WAB), Business Card (.VCF), Microsoft Office Outlook Address Book, Address Book for Current Windows User, or Comma Separated Values (.CSV).

If an Import Wizard dialog box opens to prompt you for the location of the file of the address book you selected and later for the particular fields you want to include, browse for the file and then select the fields to use before you click the Finish button. Windows displays a Contacts Import dialog box that shows you the progress of the contacts import.

4. After Windows Live Mail finishes importing the names and e-mail addresses of all the contacts in the existing address book, close the Contacts Import dialog box by clicking its OK button to return to the Windows Live Contacts window.

    Icons for all the contacts in the imported address book now appear in the Contacts window. To display a list of the full names along with e-mail addresses and business and home phone numbers in the window, click the Menus button and then select List from its drop-down menu.

5. (Optional) To filter out all contacts except for those in a particular group of contacts, click the category button (Coworkers, Family, Favorites, or Friends) under Contact in the Navigation pane.

    Coworkers, Family, Favorites, or Friends are the four predefined categories that are automatically available in the Live Contacts window. To add your own categories to this list, click the Create a New Category link at the bottom of the Navigation pane and then enter the name of the category in the text box at the top of the Create a New Category dialog box and select all the contacts you want added to this category (by clicking their names in the list box below). Then click Save.

6. When you finish filtering and viewing the contacts list with the imported contacts, click the Close button in the upper-right corner of the Windows Live Contacts window to close it.

Reading e-mail

When you use Windows Live Mail as your e-mail program, you read the messages that you receive in an area known as the Inbox. To open the Inbox in Windows Live Mail and read your e-mail, take these steps:

1. Launch Windows Live Mail (Start⇨All Programs⇨Windows Live⇨Windows Live Mail).

2. Click the Sync button on the Windows Live Mail toolbar. If you have more than one e-mail account defined for Windows Live Mail, click the Sync drop-down button and then choose All E-Mail Accounts from the drop-down menu or press F5.

    Windows Live Mail opens a connection to your mail server, where it checks for any new messages to download. New messages are then downloaded to your computer. The program also selects the Inbox view in the Navigation pane, which lists the messages in the Inbox in the Information viewer, while at the same time selecting the last message received at the top of the viewer so that details of its text are displayed in the Reading pane.

You can also open this Inbox view by clicking the Inbox button under the mail account name in the Navigation pane.

Descriptions of any new messages appear in bold in the Inbox List pane to the immediate right of the Navigation pane: Priority (indicated by an exclamation mark), Attachments (indicated by the paper clip), Flagged Messages (indicated by the flag), From, Subject, and Received (showing both the date and time that the e-mail was downloaded on your computer).

Note that messages that you haven't yet read are indicated not only by bold type, but also by a sealed-envelope icon next to the message name. Mail messages that you have read are indicated by an opened-envelope icon.

3. To read one of your new messages, click its name in the List pane of the Inbox.

   The text of the message that you select then appears in the Detail pane to the right of the List pane in the Windows Live Mail window.

   If the e-mail uses the high-priority exclamation mark icon, chances are good that you may have to reply to it right away. You can respond to the message by clicking either the Reply or the Reply All button, as spelled out in Step 7.

4. (Optional) To open the file or files attached to the e-mail message with its native program (or at least one that can open the file), click the paper-clip icon and then choose the name of the file to open in the pop-up menu. To save the attachments as separate files on your hard drive, choose Save Attachments from this pop-up menu, select the folder in which to save the files in the Save Attachments dialog box and then click Save.

5. (Optional) To print the contents of an e-mail, press Ctrl+P and then click Print in the Print dialog box.

   Sometimes, you may need to print a hard copy of the message to share with other, less fortunate workers in the office who don't have e-mail. (If they do have e-mail, forward the message to them instead, as I cover in the optional Step 8.)

6. (Optional) To save the contents of an e-mail as a separate e-mail file, choose File⇨Save As from the Classic menus (Alt+MM) to open the Save Message As dialog box. If you want to edit the filename, make your changes to the name in the File Name combo box. To save the file in a folder different from the one shown in the Save In field, position the

mouse over this field and then click the drop-down button and select a new destination on its list. Alternatively, click the Browse Folders button to expand the Save Message As dialog box and then select a new folder by using its Navigation pane. Then click the Save button.

7. (Optional) To reply to the author of the e-mail message, click the Reply button on the Windows Live Mail toolbar. To send copies of the reply to all the others copied on the original message as well, click the Reply All button instead.

   After you click one or the other of these buttons, Windows Live Mail opens a message window in which

   • The sender of the original message is listed as the recipient in the To field.

   • The subject of the original message appears in the Subject field, preceded by the term Re: (regarding).

   • The contents of the original message appear in the body of the reply beneath the heading Original Message, followed by the From, To, Date, and Subject information from the original message.

   Add the text of your reply above the text of the original message and send the reply (by pressing the Send button, Ctrl+Enter or Alt+S).

   Sometimes, in addition to or instead of replying to the original message, you need to send a copy of it to someone who wasn't listed in the Cc field. To send a copy to this person, you *forward* a copy of the original message to the new recipients of your choosing.

8. (Optional) To forward the e-mail to another e-mail address, click the Forward button on the Windows Live Mail toolbar. Then fill in the recipient information in the To field and, if applicable, the Bcc or Cc fields; type any additional text of your own above that of the original message; and send the forwarded message on its way (by clicking the Send button or pressing Ctrl+Enter or Alt+S).

   When you forward a message, Windows Mail copies the subject line and contents of the original message to a new message, which you then address and send.

 TIP If you ever open an e-mail and then don't have time to really read through it and digest the meaning, you can, if you like, have Windows Live Mail mark the message as unread to remind you to reread it when you have more time. To mark a read e-mail message as unread, choose Edit⇨Mark as Unread from the Classic menus (Alt+MM). Windows Live Mail then replaces the open-envelope icon in front of the current message with the closed-envelope icon. To temporarily hide all messages in the Inbox except those you haven't yet read, choose View⇨Show or Hide⇨Hide Read Messages from the Classic menus (Alt+MM). To later redisplay both the read and unread messages in the Inbox, you then choose View⇨Show or Hide⇨Show All Messages.

Keep in mind that as part of the security features in Windows 7, Windows Live Mail now automatically blocks the display of all pictures in incoming messages (to prevent the sender from harming your computer). If you trust the source of the message, you can display the images by clicking the note at the top of body of the e-mail to let Windows Live Mail know that you want to view the blocked pictures.

Organizing e-mail

Getting e-mail is great, but it doesn't take long for you to end up with a disorganized mess. If you're anything like me, your Windows Live Mail Inbox will end up with hundreds of messages, some of which are still unread — and all of which are lumped together in one extensive list.

Windows Live Mail makes it easy for you to arrange your e-mail in folders. To send a bunch of related messages into a new or existing folder, follow these steps:

1. Launch Windows Live Mail (Start⇨All Programs⇨Windows Live⇨Windows Live Mail) to open the Windows Live Mail window with the Inbox selected.

2. Select all the messages that you want to put in the same folder. To select a single message, click the description. To select a continuous series of messages, click the first one and hold down the Shift key as you click the last one. To click multiple messages that aren't in a series, hold down Ctrl as you click the description of each one.

3. After you select the messages that you want to move, choose Edit⇨Move To Folder from the Classic menus (Alt+MM) or simply press Ctrl+Shift+V to open the Move dialog box.

4. In the Move dialog box, click the Expand button to the immediate left of the Local Folders icon to display its subfolders (Inbox, Outbox, Sent Items, and so on) and then click the name of the subfolder into which the selected messages are to be moved. If you need to create a new folder for the selected items, click the New Folder button, type the name in the Folder Name text box, and click OK. Then click the Inbox folder icon before clicking the name of the newly created subfolder.

5. Click OK in the Move dialog box to move the messages into the selected folder.

To verify that the items are now in the correct folder, click the Folder icon in the outline (beneath the Inbox icon) that appears in the Navigation pane of the Windows Live Mail window.

Don't forget that the most basic way to organize your e-mail is by sorting all the messages in the Inbox (or any of the other Windows Live Mail folders, for that matter) on a particular field such as Subject. (The program automatically sorts on the date received.) For example, if you want to sort the e-mail in your Inbox by subject, display the Classic menus (Alt+MM) and then choose View⇨Sort By⇨ Subject.

Deleting e-mail

When you have messages (especially those unsolicited ones) that you no longer need to store on your computer hard drive, you can move those messages to the Deleted Items folder by selecting them and then pressing the Delete key (Ctrl+D). You can then get rid of them for good by right-clicking the Deleted Items icon in Navigation pane, choosing Empty 'Deleted Items' Folder from the shortcut menu that appears, and then clicking Yes in the alert box telling you that you're about to permanently delete the selected messages.

If you receive unsolicited messages from advertisers or people whose e-mail you don't want to receive again in the future, add the sender to the Blocked Senders list so that all future messages from that sender automatically go into the Junk E-Mail folder, choose Add Sender to Blocked Senders List from the same short-cut menu. You then receive an alert dialog box informing you that the person has been added to your Blocked Senders list and telling you that the sender's message has been moved to the Junk E-Mail folder. Click the OK button to close this dialog box.

If you simply want to move the unsolicited message to your Junk e-mail folder without blocking all future messages from the sender, choose Mark as Junk on the message's shortcut menu (or press Ctrl+Alt+J).

TIP

You can remove someone you've blocked from your Blocked Senders list so that you can once again get e-mail from that person. If you still have a message from the sender, right-click the message, and then choose Add Sender to Safe Senders List from the shortcut menu that appears. If you no longer have any messages from the sender, click the Menus button (the one in front of the Help button on the toolbar) and then click Safety Options to open the Safety Options dialog box. Click the Blocked Senders tab and there click the name of the sender you want to unblock in its list box; then click the Remove button and click OK.

To remove messages from the Inbox without permanently getting rid of them, select them and then press the Delete key. They instantly disappear from the Inbox window. If you ever need them again, however, you can display them by clicking the Deleted Items button in the Windows Live Mail window Navigation pane. If you find a message in the Deleted Items folder that you intended to keep, drag its message icon and drop it on the Inbox folder (or whatever other special folder you've created for your mail messages) in the Folders pane.

Messenger

Instant messaging (IM, for short) with Windows Live Messenger enables you and another person (co-worker, friend, family member, and so forth) to exchange text messages, photos, video, and audio and even play games over the Internet in real time (unlike e-mailing back and forth or playing telephone tag). IM with

Windows Live Messenger makes it easy to quickly exchange important information as well as to stay current on the latest office chitchat.

As part of installing Windows Live Messenger on your computer (having downloaded the program alone or with other applications in the Windows Live Essentials suite), you need to sign in using an e-mail account. You can sign in to Windows Live Messenger using your Windows Live ID that you use with Windows Live Mail (*see* "Mail" earlier in this part), Windows Live Hotmail or Windows Live Spaces account. And if you don't yet have any of these accounts, you can easily set up your Windows Live ID. Simply, use your Internet Explorer Web browser to visit the Windows Live login page at `http://home.live.com`, where you click the Sign Up button and follow the online instructions.

TIP

If you're planning on using instant messaging regularly, you can set up the Windows Live Messenger so that the program automatically logs you in whenever it starts. To set up automatic login, click the Show Sign In Options button (the one with the greater than symbol pointing downward to the right of the Sign In As drop-down list in the window that appears when you first launch Windows Live Messenger before you sign in). Then select the Sign Me in Automatically check box (and make sure that both the Remember Me and Remember My Password are selected) before you click the Sign In button.

After you log in to Windows Live Messenger, a window similar to the one shown in Figure 8-2 appears (except that it contains your information and not mine). Here you can customize the look and feel of the program window as well as add contacts and, of course, send and receive instant messages.

Figure 8-2

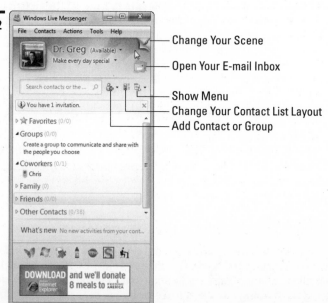

Change Your Scene

Open Your E-mail Inbox

Show Menu

Change Your Contact List Layout

Add Contact or Group

Customizing Windows Live Messenger

Windows Live Messenger makes it super easy to customize its window. You can customize the display picture, the scene (the background graphic image and colors that appear at the top of Windows Live Messenger window), as well as the personal information (including display name, your personal message, and any picture that you want displayed).

To change these settings, click the drop-down button that appears to the right of your current display name and online status (your status is usually Available when you first log in to Windows Live Messenger) and then select any of the following menu options:

- **Change Display Picture:** Click this option to open the Display Picture dialog box where you can select a new picture from among the predefined images supplied with Windows Live Messenger, take a snapshot or short video or dynamic picture (using a series of still frames) with your webcam, or go online to create a Dynamic WeeMee or to select a predefined Quebles or Kiwee display picture.

- **Change Scene:** Click this option to open the Scene dialog box, where you can select a new background graphic for the top of the Windows Live Messenger window from among those predefined or browse for a photo or image that you've saved on your computer as well as to select a new color scheme used for displaying the text in this area of the Windows Live Messenger window.

- **Change Display Name:** Click this option to open the Options dialog box with the Personal tab selected. Here you can change your display name, reword the short personal message that your contacts see (mine is "Make Every Day Special"), as well as change or select a new display picture. This tab also contains options for editing the public profile that your contacts can see when you're logged in, changing the Status options that control how long Messenger remains inactive before your status automatically changes from Available to Away, and determining whether your status automatically changes from Available to Busy when you're running a full-screen program or have turned on presentation settings. This tab also includes an option that controls whether the program automatically displays a webcam icon in the contact's message window indicating that you have a webcam (assuming that your computer is so equipped) when the contact is receiving your instant message.

Adding contacts to Windows Live Messenger

Contacts in Windows Live Messenger are the people you want to communicate with using instant messages. When you add a person to your contacts list, Windows Live Messenger automatically alerts you when that person is logged in to his version of the instant messenger program.

Windows Live Messenger makes it easy to add the contacts to your list. Simply click the Contacts button on the toolbar at the top of the window or click the Add a Contact or Group button (see Figure 8-2) and then select the Add a Contact option from the drop-down menu. Windows Live Messenger then opens a dialog box where you enter the person's instant messaging address (such as **gharvey@live.com**) in the Instant Messaging Address text box. If the contact has a mobile phone with text messaging service, you can also enter his or her cell-phone number into the Mobile Device Number text box after selecting the country in the Select Country or Region drop-down list (when entering the phone number, be sure to include the area code). You can also make the new contact a part of a particular *category* (previously known as a *group*) by selecting the category in the Add to a Category drop-down list (these categories include pre-defined categories such as Favorites, Family, and Friends as well as custom categories that you add) before you click the Next button.

After adding a person to Windows Live Messenger contacts list, the program plays an audible alert and displays a visual alert in the Windows notification area as soon as that person first logs in to his Windows Live Messenger on his computer, letting you know that that contact is now available for instant messaging. To remind you of the person's Available status, a green square icon then appears in front of the contact's name in his category in the Windows Live Messenger window (as long as the contact doesn't log off Windows Live Messenger or change his status to Appear Offline by selecting this option from the drop-down menu attached to his display name).

Instant messaging with Windows Live Messenger

To send an instant message to an available contact with Windows Live Messenger, position the mouse pointer over his or her name in the program window (displayed under the appropriate category). Then click the Send an Instant Message option on the menu that pops up to the side of the contact's display name.

Windows Live Messenger then opens a separate message window (similar to the one shown in Figure 8-3) containing the contact's name in the title bar and with the contact's display image shown at the top. At the bottom of this window, you find your display image next to a text box where you type the lines of message text you want to send to your contact. To send a line of text you've type to that person, simply press the Enter key. The moment you do, Windows Live Messenger displays your new line of text both in your message window as well as in the contact's message window.

If you want to save the conversation for future reference, click the Show Menu button to the right of the message window's toolbar and then choose Save from the drop-down menu. Windows then displays an alert dialog box letting you know that the conversation will be saved in Microsoft's Rich Text format (.rtf). After you click OK, the program displays a Save As dialog box, where you select the filename and folder in which to save the file.

Figure 8-3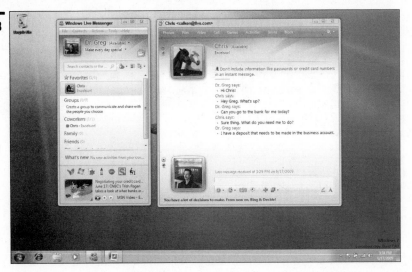

When you finish conversing with your contact, you can end the instant message session by clicking the Close button in the upper-right of the message window.

Movie Maker

You can use the Windows Live Movie Maker program to capture video and audio clips, which you can then edit and arrange into your very own movies. You can play these movie files on your computer or distribute them to family, friends, and colleagues by e-mail so that they can play them on their computers.

Launch Movie Maker by choosing Start⇨All Programs⇨Windows Live⇨Windows Live Movie Maker. Windows opens the Movie Maker window, similar to the one shown in Figure 8-4 (except that yours doesn't have any content in it).

Figure 8-4

Play button   Preview area   Collection area

The Windows Live Movie Maker window is divided into two sections:

- ✔ **Collections area** on the right side which shows thumbnails of the various still graphic images, video clips, and audio clips you add in the order in which they play in the final movie.

- ✔ **Preview area,** which displays whatever video image or clip is selected in the Collections area. You can also use this area to preview the movie that you're putting together by clicking the first thumbnail in the Collections area and then clicking the Play button located to the left of the slider under the Preview window.

Importing still and video clips into your movie

To add the media clips for your new movie to the Collections area of the Movie Maker window, you import the picture files and captured video clips you've stored in folders on the hard drive of your computer.

Simply click the Add button in the Videos and Photos section of the Home tab of the Movie Maker Ribbon (the one with the plus sign in front of the picture). Windows Live Movie Maker then opens the Add Videos and Photos dialog box, where you can then open the media library folder (usually the Pictures or Videos libraries) and select the photos or video clips you want before clicking the Open button.

TIP To add a sound file to play as the soundtrack for the movie (in addition to any audio that's captured as part of the videos clips you import), click the Add button in the Soundtrack section of the Movie Maker's Ribbon. (The Add button is the one with the plus sign in front of the music note.) The Movie Maker then opens the Add Music dialog box, where you open the library folder (usually the Music library) and then select the audio file you want to play in the background.

Arranging the clips in your movie

The Windows Live Movie Maker adds your photos and video clip media files to the Collections area in the order in which they are imported. Once imported, you can then arrange them in the Collections area in the order you want them to played in the movie (from left to right down each row).

To move a photo or video clip to a new position in the movie, drag its icon and when the black vertical bar appears before the thumbnail where you want to insert the photo or video, drop it into position by releasing the mouse button.

TIP To preview your movie in the Preview window in order from first thumbnail to last after rearranging its photos and/or video clips in the Collections area, click the first thumbnail in the Collections area before you click the Play button under the Preview window. Windows Movie Maker shows you which clip is being played in the Preview window by highlighting its thumbnail in the Collections area.

Adjusting the duration of your clips

You can modify the duration of the photos and the video clips that you add to your movie. To change the time that a particular photo is displayed in the movie, click its thumbnail in the Collections area and then click the Edit tab on the Movie Maker Ribbon. The current time the photo is displayed in the movie (in seconds) then appears in the Duration combo box in the Photo section. To lengthen or shorten this duration, enter the new number of seconds in this box or select the value from its drop-down list.

To change the duration of a video clip in the movie by modifying its starting and/or ending frame (a process referred to as *trimming*), select its thumbnail in the Collections area and then click the Trim button in the Video section of the Edit tab on the Ribbon. Movie Maker then displays the Trim tab on the Ribbon and adds trim handles to the beginning and end of the clip's slider under the Preview window. To trim the beginning of the video clip, drag the trim handle at the beginning of the slider to the right until you reach the frame that you now want to be the first one in the clip. To trim the end of the clip, drag the trim handle at the back end of the slider to the left until you reach the frame you now want to be the last one in the clip.

To preview the trimmed clip, click the Play button under the Preview window. When you're satisfied with the video edit, click the Save and Close button in the Exit section of the Trim tab. (Note, however, that trimming a video clip only changes the first and last frames that Windows Live Movie Maker plays — it does nothing destructive to the clip itself, so you can easily restore all the frames by resetting the clip so that every frame from first to last is once again played.)

Adding special effects to clips

Movie Maker includes a variety of special effects that you can apply to the clips you've added to your movie. To add a special effect to a clip in the movie project, click the Visual Effects tab on the Ribbon and then click the effect you want to apply in the Effects section.

TIP

To remove an effect from a photo or video clip, all you have to do is click the thumbnail in the Collections area and then click the blank effect icon (the first one) in the Effects section of the Visual Effects tab on the Movie Maker Ribbon.

Adding transitions

Transitions are the effects that smooth out the changeover from one photo or video clip to the next in the movie project. In Windows Live Movie Maker, you can choose from a number of transitions, including Crossfade, Slide, and Roll.

To add a transition between two clips in the movie project, click the second clip of the pair in the Collections area and then click the transition you want to apply in the Transitions section of the Visual Effects tab on the Ribbon.

To preview just the transition in the movie, simply click the Play button under the Preview window. If you want to remove a transition from between two clips, click the second of the pair in the Collections area and then click the blank transition icon (the first one) in the Transitions section of the Visual Effects tab on the Ribbon.

TIP

If you want to add a crossfade transition at the very beginning of the movie so that your movie fades from black into the first photo or scene in the initial video clip, click the first thumbnail in the Collections area and then click the Crossfade transition icon (the second one) in the Transitions section of the Visual Effects tab on the Ribbon.

Adding text to a movie clip

Windows Live Media Player enables you to add text to your movie clips. To add a caption to a particular photo or video clip in the project, select its thumbnail in the Collections area and then click the Text Box button on the Edit tab in the Text section of the Ribbon.

Movie Maker then adds a text box to the near center of the selected clip in the Preview pane, where you can type your text. You can use the buttons in the Font section of the Edit tab to change the text's font, font size, and color as well as to add attributes such as bold and italics.

To resize the text box so that all the text you enter into it appears, drag one of the four sizing handles at the corners of the box. To move the text in the frame, position the mouse pointer somewhere on the text box's border (outside the sizing handles) and then, when the pointer becomes a cross with four arrowheads, drag the text box and drop it in its new position in the frame.

Publishing the final movie

When you finish all your movie edits and are satisfied with the final version, you can save your movie project and then either upload it to the MSN Soapbox on the Web or convert it into a movie that can be played on a DVD player or some portable device. To save your project, click the Movie Maker button and then click the Save item, press Ctrl+S, or click the Save button on Quick Access toolbar.

To publish the movie to the MSN Soapbox (Microsoft's version of YouTube where you can share your videos on the Internet), click the Publish button in the Make Movie section of the Home tab on the Movie Maker Ribbon. Then enter a movie title in the Title text box and add any *tags* (which are basically descriptive words for identifying the movie in a search) in the Description text box. Select a category for the movie in the Category drop-down list and, if you don't want everyone on the Web to see the movie, select Hidden in the Permission drop-down list. Finally, click the I Agree to the Terms of Use and Soapbox Safety Tips check box before you click the Publish button.

To publish your movie project in a file format for playback on your computer or another standalone device, click the Output button in the Make Movie section of the Home tab on the Movie Maker Ribbon. Then, click the Windows Media DVD Quality (.WMV) item for playback on your computer or a DVD player or click Windows Media Portable Device (.WMV) for playback on a portable device such as your cellphone.

Movie Maker then opens the Output Movie dialog box, where you select the folder where you want your movie saved and designate its filename before you click the Save button. After Windows finishes outputting and saving your movie, an alert dialog box indicating that the movie is complete appears. To play the movie with the Windows Media Player, click the Open button.

To close the alert dialog box without playing your movie and return to the Windows Live Movie Maker window, click the Close button instead. Then, after closing the Windows Live Movie Maker window, you can test your finished movie in the Windows Media Player: Simply open the folder where the movie is saved and double-click the file icon to play the movie with Windows Media Player.

Use the Windows DVD Maker program when you want to burn your final published movie to a DVD so that it can then be played on any standalone DVD player as well as in any computer's DVD drive. (*See* Part 6 for details.)

Photo Gallery

The Windows Live Photo Gallery enables you to easily keep track of and manage the digital photos and videos that you save on your computer. To open the Windows Live Photo Gallery window, which will look similar to the one shown in Figure 8-5, choose Start⇨All Programs⇨Windows Live⇨Windows Live Photo Gallery.

When you first open the Windows Live Photo Gallery window, the All Photos and Videos link is selected in its Navigation pane on the left so that thumbnails of all the photo and video media files on your computer are displayed, grouped by the date they were taken.

Keep in mind that you can change the orientation of any photo displayed in the Gallery, which is handy if you rotated the camera 90 degrees to the left or right so as to fit a tall image in the picture. Simply click the Rotate Counterclockwise button in the image controls at the bottom of the window or press Ctrl+comma (,) to rotate counterclockwise. To rotate clockwise, click the Rotate Clockwise button or press Ctrl+period (.).

Figure 8-5

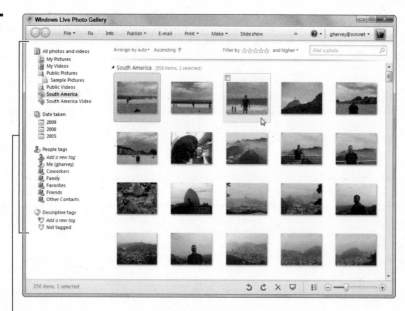

Navigation pane

TIP Drag the zoom slider that appears in the lower-right corner of the Windows Live Photo Gallery window right and left to quickly make all the media files' thumbnails larger or smaller.

To filter which media files are displayed in the Windows Live Photo Gallery window, expand the desired category link in the Navigation pane by clicking the Expand button (the triangle pointing to the right) in front of the link name and then clicking the filtering criterion in the list. For example, to display only the pictures and videos taken on March 23, 2009, in the Windows Live Photo Gallery, I would first click 2009 in the Date Taken category and then click March followed by Mar 23, Monday.

To change the view details about the photos and videos displayed in the Photo Gallery along with their thumbnails, click the View Details button (the one to the immediate left of the zoom slider at the bottom) or press Ctrl+0 (zero). To return to just the thumbnail display, click this button (which is now View Thumbnails) a second time or simply press Ctrl+0 again.

The toolbar at the top of the Windows Live Photo Gallery window contains the following buttons that you can use to manage your photo and video media files:

- **File:** Performs all file-related tasks on selected files, including renaming, copying, and deleting them as well as adding new folders to the Gallery, importing images from a scanner or camera, and syncing images and videos to a compatible portable device.

- **Fix:** Opens a selected photo in a special Gallery window containing controls for adjusting the image's color and exposure, cropping the image, and fixing red eye.

- **Info:** Displays a Reader pane on the right side of the Windows Live Photo Gallery window containing a thumbnail with all vital information about a photo or video, such as ratings, search tags, and, in the case of photos, a caption.

- **Publish:** Opens a drop-down menu with options for publishing selected photos to your blog or to online albums on the Windows Live Web site or some other photo-sharing site such as Snapfish or Flickr.

- **E-mail:** Opens a new e-mail in Windows Live Mail with the selected media files attached. When you select photos to attach to a new message, Windows first opens an Attach Files dialog box, where you can select the size of the images in the Photo Size drop-down menu — very helpful in controlling file size — before clicking the Attach button. (Your choices here are Smaller: 640 x 480; Small: 800 x 600; Medium: 1024 x 768; Large: 1280 x 1024; or No Compression.)

✔ **Print:** Prints all selected photos in the Gallery or to open the Order Prints dialog box, where you can select an online printing company from which you can order professional prints of your photos.

✔ **Make:** Opens a drop-down menu from which you can choose any of the following:

- *Create a Panoramic Photo:* Use this option to stitch together two or more photos to create a composite picture (assuming that you've selected a series of photos that cover the same panorama).

- *Make a Movie:* This option lets you import the files into a new movie project in the Windows Live Movie Maker. (*See* "Importing still and video clips into your movie," earlier in this part.)

- *Make a Blog Post:* Use this option to open the Windows Live Writer and add the selected media files to a new post that you can then upload to your blog.

- *Burn a DVD:* This option lets you add the selected media files to an Add Pictures and Video to the DVD screen in the Windows DVD Maker. (*See* "Windows DVD Maker" in Part 6 for details.)

- *Burn a Data CD:* This option lets you burn the selected media files to a CD or DVD data disc in your computer's CD/DVD drive using a program such as Windows Media Player.

✔ **Slideshow:** Use this option to display the selected media files in a full-screen slideshow. To control the playback during the slideshow or exit it, position the mouse pointer near the bottom of the screen to display the controls. Click the Pause button to pause the playback and the Exit button to return to the Windows Live Photo Gallery on the Windows 7 desktop.

Keep in mind that you can select photo and media files in the Windows Live Photo Gallery by positioning the mouse pointer over each thumbnail and then clicking the check box that appears in the upper-left corner of the thumbnail. Photos and videos selected in this manner then remain selected (indicated by the blue highlighting around their thumbnail images), enabling you to scroll through the other thumbnails adding others, until you click the mouse in a blank area between the thumbnails. The great thing about this method of selecting media files (as opposed to Ctrl+clicking, Shift+clicking, or dragging through the thumbnails) is that you can deselect a media file simply by positioning the mouse over its thumbnail and then clicking its check box again to clear its check mark *without* automatically deselecting all the other selected media files in the Gallery.

Windows Logo Key Shortcuts

A great many of the keyboards connected to computers running Windows 7 are equipped with a special Windows logo key ( ). This key is located to the immediate left of the Alt key on the bottom row of the keyboard with the spacebar and contains a colorless Windows logo that appears to me like a waving rally flag with four distinct parts. (Who knows what it reminds you of?)

The table that follows gives you a list of all the great keyboard shortcuts that Windows 7 supports for those of you with keyboards blessed with the special Windows logo key.

Windows Logo Key Shortcuts in Windows 7

Press This	To Do This
	Display or hide the Windows 7 Start menu (same as clicking the Start button on the Windows taskbar)
+Pause/Break	Open the System Control Panel window
+D	Toggle between displaying the Windows 7 desktop by hiding all open windows and then redisplaying all minimized windows (same as clicking the Show Desktop button on the Windows taskbar)
+M	Minimize all open windows on the desktop
+Shift+M	Redisplay all minimized windows on the desktop
+E	Open Computer in an Explorer window
+F	Open Search Results in an Explorer window
+L	Lock the computer or switch users
+R	Open the Run dialog box
+T	Cycle through programs open on the Windows taskbar
+Tab	Cycle through open windows in Flip 3-D
Ctrl+ +Tab	Enable you to cycle through open windows in Flip 3-D using your arrow keys
+spacebar	Preview the desktop by making all open windows transparent except for their outlines

Press This	To Do This
+U	Open the Ease of Access Center Control Panel window
+X	Open the Windows Mobility Center
+[number key]	Open the window attached to the Quick Launch button on the taskbar corresponding to the number you press, so that when you press +1, Windows opens the Internet Explorer window because Internet Explorer is the first Quick Launch button (to the immediate right of the Start button) and pressing +2 opens the Libraries Window Explorer window because the Windows Explorer button is the second Quick Launch button on the Windows 7 taskbar

Index

Notes